Nineteenth-Century Europe

Nineteenth-Century Europe

A Cultural History

HANNU SALMI

polity

First published in 2008 by Polity Press

Polity Press
65 Bridge Street
Cambridge CB2 1UR, UK

Polity Press
350 Main Street
Malden, MA 02148, USA

ISBN-13: 978-0-7456-4359-5
ISBN-13: 978-0-7456-4360-1(pb)

A catalogue record for this book is available from the British Library.

Typeset in 11 on 13 pt Bembo by
Servis Filmsetting Limited, Stockport, Cheshire.
Printed and bound in Great Britain by MPG Books Limited, Bodmin, Cornwall

The publisher has used its best endeavours to ensure that the URLs for external websites referred to in this book are correct and active at the time of going to press. However, the publisher has no responsibility for the websites and can make no guarantee that a site will remain live or that the content is or will remain appropriate.

Every effort has been made to trace all copyright holders, but if any have been inadvertently overlooked the publishers will be pleased to include any necessary credits in any subsequent reprint or edition.

For further information on Polity, visit our website: www.polity.co.uk

Contents

Acknowledgements

In his *Passions of the Soul*, the French philosopher René Descartes argued that all passions are based on wonder. This book has offered me ample possibilities for wondering. The century that is only a few generations away from us is both strange and familiar. The 19th century has often been described as a century of rising factory pipes and grey industrial cities, and as a cradle of modern culture, but the era has many faces. This book pays special attention to the experiences of contemporaries: from the fear of steaming engines to the longing for a pre-industrial past, from the idle calmness of bourgeois life to the awakening consumerism of department stores, from curious exoticism to increasing xenophobia, and from optimistic visions of the future to expectations of an approaching end.

The journey into the perplexities of a century has been long, and would never have been realized without the support of my friends at the Department of Cultural History at the University of Turku. Founded in 1972, the department is one of the oldest academic units in cultural history, if not the oldest one, in Europe. There has always been a special interest in the cultural history of the 19th century, modernity and popular culture within the department, especially in the work of Keijo Virtanen and, later,

Kari Immonen, Ritva Hapuli, Kari Kallioniemi and Anne Ollila. I warmly thank you for all your support and assistance! This book has been written during the last six years, and started with the aim of writing a concise survey of the 19th century. I wish to thank especially Kalle Pihlainen who translated most of the text into fluent English several years ago. A cultural historian himself, Kalle has been an excellent commentator, giving valuable advice throughout the project. The manuscript has been completely revised, expanded and updated during the last year, and Kalle has shown incredible flexibility in smoothing my extensions to the text.

I would also like to thank Hanne Koivisto, Katriina Mäkinen, Sakari Ollitervo and Heli Paalumäki for their inspiring comments and suggestions. I am especially grateful to Katriina who also offered the possibility of starting this project as a course for the Centre for Extension Studies at the University of Turku.

Hannu Salmi
Turku, March 2008

Introduction

Let us not be deceived: that vestment of black which the men of our time wear is a terrible symbol; before coming to this, the armour must have fallen piece by piece and the embroidery flower by flower. Human reason has overthrown all illusions; but it bears in itself sorrow, in order that it may be consoled.[1]

So the French author Alfred de Musset (1810–57) described the emotions at the start of the nineteenth century in his *Confession of a Child of the Century* (*La confession d'un enfant du siècle*). When de Musset's book appeared in 1836, it was against the background of the Great Revolution in France and its distressing consequences. De Musset saw the new men's fashion, the black suit which had lost the elegance and pageantry of earlier centuries, as a symbol of the times. In the age of the physical sciences and industrialization, beauty was replaced by a calculating rationality that was found more appropriate. In historical literature and imagination, the nineteenth century is indeed portrayed more often as black and white or grey, as the era of great socio-economic structural changes: industrial production revolutionized the economy, urbanization accelerated, and the working class and the women's rights movement were born. The nineteenth century has also been called the century of 'isms'.

Intellectual and artistic movements like nationalism, conservatism, socialism, liberalism, Darwinism, realism and impressionism have become almost indispensable elements in the perception of the century. In traditional cultural historical accounts, the century has appeared not only as a period of ideas and art but also as one of growth in material well-being, and as the triumph of science and technology. My aim is, instead, to construct a picture of another kind of nineteenth century – not one that would forget the significance of Darwin or Marx, for example, but one that provides room for the more commonplace as well as for more concrete cultural phenomena, and that would at the same time listen to how contemporaries perceived their past, present and future.

I have, in this endeavour, attempted to see culture broadly: it is not limited to the worlds of science, art and religion, but embraces ways of life as mental, material and social practices, also tackling them on the level of ways of thinking, mentalities and emotions. In 1973, the anthropologist Clifford Geertz wrote in his *Interpretation of Cultures* that culture can be defined as webs of significance.[2] Obviously, the Geertzian idea carries overly strong implications: the metaphor of the 'web' solidifies culture that is, instead, in continuous flow. It might also make us forget that culture is not outside or around humans, as codes or structures of signification. A meaning is neither a knot nor a thread of the web: it is a relation. This is why meanings can never be separated from the people of the past and their cultural products. It is crucial to stress that culture is neither just a discursive fabrication nor something that can be fully comprehended by emphasizing the immaterial processes of signification. A cultural history of nineteenth-century Europe should pay attention to the agents of history that spun their webs of significance and also changed them;[3] to those social practices that connected and disconnected people of the past; and to that tangible, concrete, bodily world in which the people of the century lived and experienced their surroundings, both real and imagined.

Fundamentally, cultural history means the study of relations. It may be seen as a study of the way in which the people of the past interacted with their environment. Even emotions were a part of this dialogue: the people of the past responded to the phenomena of their time – perhaps differently from the way in which we might. Meanings, signs, symbols and representations are, and were, in constant flow, under circulation and change, in a perpetual process of becoming. Still, there are slower rhythms, deeply rooted assemblages, like the gender system or religious beliefs, that need to be considered over a much longer time span.[4]

Given this comprehensive approach, it is clear that it would be difficult to examine any historical period in a single compact and coherent presentation. For this reason, I must admit that my presentation will not cover everything. We can certainly locate social, and perhaps even national, particularities in various dimensions of culture and thus construct generalizations, yet the differences are also significant. These differences can be, for instance, internal to communities as well as geographical. We can hardly assume that generalizations about nineteenth-century culture would apply simultaneously to that vast geographical area that Europe is, reaching from the shores of the Arctic Ocean to those of the Mediterranean, from the boulevards of Lisbon to the streets of Moscow. European cultural multiplicity was as concrete a reality in the nineteenth century as it is today – perceiving the distinctive features is therefore important. Let us only think of the relation between the urban and rural populations during the century. The majority of Europeans lived in the countryside throughout the nineteenth century and their lifestyle differed enormously from that of the inhabitants of urban centres like St Petersburg, Paris, Berlin and London.

Another absorbing question is the temporal discrepancy be tween historical processes. Although genetically oriented historians have a tendency to simplify the processes of the past by stating, for example, that the printing press was invented in the 1450s and film in the 1890s, such rough approximations should not be understood as universal or even pan European. It took a long time for the cultural impact of printed books or of films to extend over Europe. Innovations can spread slowly and receive local meanings from the particular dialogue specific to each area. The significance of this regional variance is demonstrated well by the fact that Enlightenment thought and the Copernican worldview arrived simultaneously in Latin America in the eighteenth century, despite the fact that Copernicus' *De revolutionibus orbium coelestium* had originally appeared as early as 1543.[5] In the same vein, we can follow the thinking of Wolfgang Schivelbusch to claim that railway travel changed European perceptions of time and space in the mid-nineteenth century.[6] The break may indeed have been accompanied by a mental change, yet it is hardly likely that the spread of railways in central Europe affected the perceptions of time and space of those living further afield. In addition to being a technical innovation, the railway was also an issue of experience and perceptions, and thus also had a subject, a horizon of experience situated in time and space. For this reason alone, observations cannot be extended to include all Europeans in the nineteenth century. We should also bear in mind that all cultural influence did not travel from centre to periphery, but was, rather, a matter of interaction. Central Europe was not self-evidently a source of innovations: in the field of forest protection, for example, many impulses came from Scandinavia.

Temporality is also an important starting point in another sense. We may well ask why a cultural history of the nineteenth century needs to be written at all: is a century a meaningful temporal unit? Comparing the situation in Europe at the end of the eighteenth century to that at the beginning of the twentieth, we can only conclude that changes during that century were tremendous. The nineteenth century cannot be forced into a brief overview, the particulars of which would be valid from the era of the Napoleonic Wars to the decadent atmosphere of the *fin de siècle*. Writing a history of the nineteenth century becomes meaningful only when the period is seen as an open-ended process of change, rather than a closed entity; a process with roots extending far into the past and effects felt to our present day. The task for the historian could be to explain why European culture was so different at the beginning of the twentieth century from the way it had been a hundred years earlier. The paradox lies, however, in the fact that even if the nineteenth century itself is viewed as a vague historical unit, an account of it must have – as Aristotle already revealed in his *Poetics* – both a beginning and an end. In this book, I have extended the examination beyond the obvious temporal markers.

Traditionally, the nineteenth century has been seen as defined by two historical points whose meaning is incontrovertible: the Great Revolution in France (1789) and the First World War (1914–18). Also, in this study, the emphasis is on the period between the end of the eighteenth century and the beginning of the twentieth. In some cases, the origins must, however, be traced quite far into the past because previous centuries were strongly present in the nineteenth century. On the level of lifestyles, emotions and mentalities, the horizon of understanding sometimes needs to be located beyond the limited confines of the immediate moment and even those of the fairly recent past.

In accounts of the early nineteenth century, the aftermath of the Great Revolution in France often rises powerfully into view. Contemporaries felt themselves to be living in an age of transition, a watershed between the past and future: an epoch was changing. In the already mentioned work by Alfred de Musset, this conflicting experience is interestingly summarized:

> Three elements entered into the life which offered itself to these children: behind them a past forever destroyed, still quivering on its ruins with all the fossils of centuries of absolutism; before them the aurora of an immense horizon, the first gleams of the future; and between these two worlds – like the ocean which separates the Old World from the New – something vague and floating, a troubled sea filled with wreckage, traversed from time to time by some distant sail or some ship trailing thick clouds of smoke; the present, in a word, which separates the past from the future, which is neither the one nor the other, which resembles both, and where one can not know whether, at each step, one treads on living matter or on dead refuse.[7]

De Musset's interpretation speaks of a break between the past and future. In contemporary perspective, the change was so powerful that the 'new generation' no longer felt any connection to the past, yet had not intentionally begun to build a future of its own. Interestingly enough, de Musset mentions America, which undoubtedly shimmered in the minds of the young Europeans. In between, however, lay an ocean full of the shipwrecked: the victims of political and economic upheavals. In mentioning the steamer that leaves its 'thick clouds of smoke', de Musset is also referring to industrialization. Technological change intensified the feeling of a break from the past. It is no accident that it is a steam vessel that sails the 'troubled sea filled with wreckage', the sea separating the old world from the new.

Although contemporary experience of change is certainly not sufficient to justify the temporal limits of a historical presentation, past agents can be argued to have acted on the basis of their awareness of the epoch. An investigation of the mental landscape is meaningful also because the cultural conventions as well as the patterns of thought and feeling by which Europeans lived changed so greatly. Along with increasing urbanization, ways of life and everyday customs also changed. New, urban forms of culture, an urban imagination and new forums for consumption were conceived. The modern world was born in another sense too: nationalism took firm hold in European consciousness. While patriotic feelings were of course already familiar in the eighteenth century, modern nationalism only began to take form with the Napoleonic Wars. National solidarity was perhaps largely imagined, yet national projects were an insurmountable historical phenomenon. The idea of a common past and the utopian dream of impending national harmony inspired artists and authors throughout Europe.

Where should an examination of the nineteenth century end, then? The marker cannot be set at the year 1900, although contemporaries reacted strongly to the turn of the century. In central Europe the *fin de siècle* / end of the century had already been a topic of debate for several decades. It referred above all to the interpretation of the decline and degeneration of western culture. While the phenomena occurring at the end of the nineteenth century were viewed pessimistically, the new century was expected to bring something better. It is believed that the author Émile Zola had spoken of the *fin de siècle* as early as 1886, and the term came to be better recognized from the newspaper *Le Fin de Siècle*, edited by Édouard Dujardin between 1890 and 1909.[8] When the century actually changed, nothing epoch-making happened. A fireball that many took as foretelling the end of the world was, however, seen in Scandinavia in March 1899: the so-called Bjurböle meteorite fell into the Gulf of Finland, in a bay near the town of Porvoo and, according to accounts by contemporaries, caused buildings to shake to their foundations as far as Helsinki and Tallinn.[9] On New Year's Day an exceptionally strong thunderstorm raged in Paris. The Finnish soprano Aino Ackté wrote in her memoirs: 'It awakened me at midnight, at twelve o'clock.

The sky was aflame, the house shook.'[10] In addition to the thunder, the boom of cannons and thousands of fireworks were to be heard from the city.

As always at the turn of a century, contemporaries were confused by mathematics. Did the twentieth century commence at the beginning of the year 1900 or at the beginning of 1901? Pope Leo XIII, who turned ninety in 1900, was convinced that the new century would not begin until 1 January 1901: since the year nil does not exist, a hundred years would not be up until the year 1900 was behind. Most Europeans celebrated a year earlier, however. In the great cities of central Europe, in Paris, London and Berlin, celebrations were unprecedentedly boisterous, but this enthusiasm was not found everywhere. In Finland, under Russian rule at the time, it was a bleak period. February 1899 saw the beginning of the first period of oppression during which Russia tightened its political hold. In Vyborg, near the eastern border of Finland, life was 'calm, almost silent'. Candles were placed on window sills, church bells were ringing, and people gathered at the town square to sing Martin Luther's hymn 'A Safe Stronghold Our God Is Still' and the Finnish national anthem, 'Maamme' ('Our Country').[11] If celebrations in Finland were more serious than usual, those in Russia were still to come. Imperial Russia, following the Julian calendar, stepped into the new century thirteen days later.

The turn of the century is, of course, purely a matter of numbers. A sense of being at a turning point could have been part of it but, in the end, epochs changed locally. In Finland the February Manifesto of 1899 marked an important milestone, noted and understood by contemporaries and highlighted in later historical research. In Great Britain, on the other hand, an indisputable turning point was the death of Queen Victoria in 1901: the Victorian period, which had started as early as 1837, ended with King Edward's succession to the throne. Lasting sixty-four years, Queen Victoria's reign imprinted the whole century in Great Britain and must not be overlooked in writing a cultural history of the nineteenth century.

Those contemporaries who pessimistically called the end of the century the *fin de siècle* were forced to admit that no new world came, even though the old century had been laid to rest. In fact, many of the phenomena that had been criticized continued past the turn of the century and even to the First World War. For this reason, it is natural to carry accounts of nineteenth-century culture through to the catastrophe known as the 'Great War'. Viewed after the epoch-making war, the turn-of-the-century world was given the name *la belle époque*, the beautiful age. Throughout the nineteenth century, the industrial society had gnawed away at the stultified foundations of the old class society, yet it was the First World War that marked the decisive crisis for the social structure and ways of life that had predominated during the nineteenth century. On the other hand, the war also led to the birth of new, small nation-states, obviously impacting on the cultural scene. At the same time, the position of the great European powers was weakened culturally as colonial and imperialist ties to other continents began to tear.

The watershed created by the First World War has undoubtedly affected our understanding of the nineteenth century. After the war, the century was 'nostalgized' to such an extent that it came to be portrayed as an idyllic world that had been lost. In this embellished yet fragile image, *la belle époque* was still a patriarchal world ruled by the bourgeoisie and landed aristocracy. Some cracks no doubt existed, but the emancipated women of the 1920s with their threat to masculine supremacy were still to come, as was the October Revolution which was to greatly alter European consciousness. Numerous descriptions of the bygone world can be found in twentieth- century literature and films. It was not, of course, simply the case of a mythological nineteenth century being constructed. Behind it lay a genuine experience, felt especially by members of genteel families. One of the finest literary depictions of the subject is Giuseppe Tomasi di Lampedusa's *The Leopard* (*Il gattopardo*, 1958), which later gained more fame in Luchino Visconti's cinematic rendition. The novel ends in a scene where the main character, Prince Salina, don Fabrizio, exits the historical stage: there is no room for an old aristocrat in the new world. At the moment of his death, don Fabrizio ponders on how different the world will be for his grandson:

> It was useless to try and avoid the thought, but the last of Salina was really he himself, this gaunt giant now dying on a hotel balcony. For

the significance of a noble family lies entirely in its traditions, that is in its vital memories; and he was the last to have any unusual memories, anything different from those of other families. Fabrizietto would only have banal ones like his schoolfellows, of snacks, of spiteful little jokes against teachers, horses bought with an eye more than to price than quality; and the meaning of his name would change more and more to empty pomp, embittered by the gadly thought that others could outdo him in outward show.[12]

In the imagination of the 'gaunt giant' don Fabrizio, the era had already changed. He would be the last of the leopards. The new democracy had brought the feudal class society to a crisis, and the descendants of the family would not experience their lives as he had. 'The Beautiful Age' has become an object of nostalgia in Giuseppe Tomasi di Lampedusa's *The Leopard*, a lost world which can never be recovered – except by means of fiction.

I have attempted to write the cultural history of the nineteenth century from a perspective that would take into account contemporary experiences and the horizons of those like don Fabrizio, even though it is clear that generalizations can never be avoided and that the particularity of the past seems impossible to grasp. The variety of past perceptions can never be fully captured; more detailed and focused studies are needed and, to be sure, there already exists a great deal of recent scholarship that sheds light on to those darkened corners of history that cannot come to the fore in concise surveys of the century. I have tried to write this portrait in a monographic way, by using primary sources, especially literary examples, novels, poems, diaries, letters and newspaper columns, in order to reflect on the contemporary experience. These excerpts are not only for relief or to illustrate the more general claims. Rather they provide a route to the feelings and imagination of historical agents. At the same time they highlight the contradictions and multiple interpretations that the otherness of the past evokes.

My examination begins with industrialization, which is investigated from the vantage point of its cultural impact as well as that provided by the emotions of those who experienced it. This approach continues in the second chapter, dealing with the nineteenth-century revolution in transportation that greatly altered the conceptions of time and space held by Europeans. Paradoxical as it may sound, the age of industrial revolution laid special emphasis on the problems of creativity, originality and individuality, which crystallized in the contemporary conception of art. This will be discussed in the third chapter. Although my aim is not to construct a comprehensive picture of the myriad ideologies afoot in the nineteenth century, the fourth chapter is devoted to nationalism, the significance of which continues to our present day, not only as a political but also as a cultural phenomenon. Other themes are the history of the family and the home (chapter 5), the history of urbanization and consumption (chapter 6), the breakthrough of mechanical reproduction, especially photography and the cinema (chapter 7), and colonial culture (chapter 8). In the last chapter I aim to construct a picture of the close of the century, the *fin de siècle*, its worldview and conceptions of human nature.

In addition to these contours, there are underlying themes or threads that run throughout the book. The culture of the nineteenth century could not be portrayed without paying attention to science and scholarly work. This thread runs all the way from the first chapter, which presents the scientific and technological accomplishments that paved the way to industrialization, to the final chapters, which delve into the fields of psychology and medicine that shaped the western imagination of body and soul during the last decades of the century. Another underlying feature that surfaces along the way is religion. Even though the eighteenth-century Enlightenment had already criticized the power and dominance of the Church, religious views and practices formed an essential part of nineteenth-century life, both in the cities and in the countryside. It can be argued that in the age of rationality there was a persistent temptation to think and wonder about the irrational and the transcendental. At a time when industrialization moved forward, the bourgeoisie devoured gothic novels and horror stories, fascinated by a world beyond sensory perception.

One of the great dividing lines in the history of Europe is inevitably the Great Revolution of France in 1789. From a religious perspective, the revolution seemed to be a backlash. The Viscount François-René de Chateaubriand wrote a compelling, overwhelming portrait of the great change in his memoirs, *Mémoires d'outre tombe*. Chateaubriand saw himself as a child of two ages. He was brought up in a feudal castle in Combourg, Brittany, and witnessed the revolutionary struggles in Paris; he hunted with the last king of France and shook hands with George Washington, but he never accepted the closing of churches after 1789 and became one of the leading conservatives of his times. He saw the Great Revolution as a break that separated the old world from the new. He expressed this rupture in a way that can well accompany readers of this book into the century that Chateaubriand did not see end: 'Now, my reader, you may continue. Cross that bloody torrent that irrevocably and eternally divides the Old World, which you come from, and the New World, on the threshold of which you will yet die.'[13]

1

Industrialization: Economy and Culture

In his short story 'A Day in the Country' (1881), Guy de Maupassant describes a bourgeois Parisian family on an excursion to the tranquillity of the countryside. After the city ruined by industry, the family enjoys the innocence of nature: 'there was sweet content and salutary refreshment to be had now that they could at last breathe a purer air which had not swept up black smoke from the factories or fumes from the sewage-pits'.[1] Although industry brought material well-being, it affected people's lives in many ways, even the manner in which surrounding reality was perceived and understood. Economic change affected not only the way in which people related to nature but also, as Maupassant's short story indicates, their views on technology. The nineteenth century can be seen as the beginning of the industrial age, yet at the same time it was the starting point for our modern western emphasis on technology. Maupassant's short story appeared, however, at a time when the effects of economic and technological changes had become readily observable and their relation to the production of material well-being had already become problematic.

When the short story was written in the 1880s, *fin de siècle* pessimism was already lifting its head. At that stage industrialization had a centennial history behind it, at least in the British Isles and in western Europe, for example in France and, to some extent, in Spain.[2] Industrialization can be seen to have started at the end of the eighteenth century but the structural changes it involved spread slowly on the European stage.[3] They did not really arrive in eastern Europe, Scandinavia, Greece or Italy until the latter half of the nineteenth century, or even later.[4] With industrialization, technological progress and research found an even more significant role in European societies than before and images associated with machines gained more ground. The picture was not just one of light and joy. The harmful effects of machines and of the tyranny of mechanization were also recognized. These dreams and fears concerning machine culture are part of the cultural inheritance left by industrialization.

Generally speaking, the so-called Industrial Revolution signifies a series of events beginning in eighteenth-century England that rapidly spread to continental Europe after the turn of the century. The term 'the Industrial Revolution' was not first used – as is often claimed – by Friedrich Engels in 1845 but probably by the French economist Adolphe Blanqui as early as 1837. For historians the term was late in coming, appearing first in *Lectures on the Industrial Revolution* (1884), an essay based on lectures given at Oxford in 1880–81 by Arnold Toynbee.[5] As a concept 'revolution' is misleading, however, since it suggests suddenness and rupture. Industrialization had a long pre-history, and its spread across Europe and the entire globe has, in the end, been a long and multifaceted process.

A central theoretician of industrialism and advocate of free enterprise was the Scottish economist Adam Smith who presented his most important theory in his *Wealth of Nations*, published in 1776. According to Smith's argument, economy is subject to laws akin to those of nature, which guide it regardless of the intentions of individual people. Supply, he argued, is defined by demand and the realities involved in production. The essential question in organizing economic activity was the division of labour. In his well-known example, Smith illustrates the significance of the division of labour from the point of view of productivity. If the production of pins is organized so that a single employee carries out all the phases involved in the work, the worker will complete only twenty pins in a day. When the labour involved is divided into eighteen stages, ten employees can produce as many as 48,000 pins per day.[6] The idea of dividing the work process has been extremely influential, and its application has not been limited to industrial activity. Cultural production was also to utilize this principle so that more goods could be produced than before with less labour involved. One is reminded of the elder Alexandre Dumas's (1802–70) early 'book factory'. Dumas managed a workshop, in which the author only indicated the main storylines and assistants completed the story.[7]

The pioneer of industrialization was England, whose political stability at the end of the eighteenth century provided better conditions for focusing on changes in the economy than those to be found in central Europe, still shaken by the Great Revolution in France. The decisive factor turned out to be investment in new kinds of technology, not only in new manufacturing solutions but also in new power sources. The progressive patent law in England also guaranteed suitable protection for technological advances. As early as 1709, Abraham Darby had found that coke could be used instead of wood as fuel in smelting iron. Considering the raw materials available on the island state, this was a significant discovery, greatly improving the conditions for producing metal as well as for exploring other technological solutions. In addition to the raw material question, the development of faster manufacturing processes was a central issue to economic life. In 1768, James Hargreaves invented the spinning machine *Spinning Jenny*. With it, an employer needed to employ only one person where ten had previously been needed. When technical solutions came to include a new power source – the steam engine built under the direction of James Watt – the conditions for fast industrial production were met. Technology had not, however, been the main impetus in this process. The market had grown quickly along with the flourishing economy, creating a need for more efficient production and thus a motive for the application of these technological innovations.

The industrial process gave workshop owners the opportunity of reducing the amount of employees to a minimum while at the same time making even quicker profits. In the long term, this meant less expensive commodities, wider markets and an increase in industrial employment. Employees began to gather in the early industrial centres: society began to take on a new form. An interesting description of the early industrial society is to be found at the beginning of French author Victor Hugo's novel *Les Misérables* (1862). Hugo describes the small town of Montreuil-sur-Mer, where the glass industry began to bloom in the 1810s due to the efforts of a kindly factory owner, Father Madeleine:

> Thanks to the rapid progress of the industry which he had so admirably re-constructed, M. sur M. had become a rather important centre of trade. Spain, which consumes a good deal of black jet, made enormous purchases there each year. M. sur M. almost rivalled London and Berlin in this branch of commerce. Father Madeleine's profits were such, that at the end of the second year he was able to erect a large factory, in which there were two vast workrooms, one for the men, and the other for women. Any one who was hungry could present himself there, and was sure of finding employment and bread. Father Madeleine required of the men good will, of the women pure morals, and of all, probity. He had separated the workrooms in order to separate the sexes, and so that the women and girls might remain discreet. On this point he was inflexible. It was the only thing in which he was in a manner intolerant. He was all the more firmly set on this severity, since M. sur M., being a garrison town, opportunities for corruption abounded. However, his coming had been a boon, and his presence was a godsend. Before Father Madeleine's arrival, everything had languished in the country; now everything lived with a healthy life of toil. A strong circulation warmed everything and penetrated everywhere. Slack seasons and wretchedness were unknown. There was no pocket so obscure that it had not a little money in it; no dwelling so lowly that there was not some little joy within it.[8]

Although Victor Hugo's *Les Misérables* depicts the unfortunates, the galley prisoner Jean Valjean and others rejected by society, he constructs an ideal of a benevolent, socially minded industrial tycoon at the beginning of the novel. For Hugo, industrialization had led to the restructuring of the world: the tiny Montreuil-sur-Mer could now compete even with London or Berlin. The old division into centres and peripheries was no longer valid since the new economy had made it possible to achieve prosperity anywhere. Father Madeleine represents the first generation of French industrialists that began to build well-being in a country ruined by the Napoleonic Wars. Madeleine is not, however, egotistically self-serving. He cares for his employees although his expectations are not limited to their labour: he expects moral and upright behaviour of them. To counterbalance this, Madeleine has built two schools and a safe-home for the town, as well as expanded the small infirmary. He has also established a subsidy for 'old and infirm workmen'. Undoubtedly Hugo is correct in showing industry as having brought well-being to many regions, at least in the long run. Even so, Father Madeleine is an ideal only. In reality, few patrons looked after the community or their employees. Hugo's description is correct in its focus on legal security: the workers in Montreuil-sur-Mer had no more legal rights than those elsewhere. In the end, everything depended on the kindness of the employer.

Perhaps it is Hugo's aim at the beginning of *Les Misérables* to show the way the world could have been if those in charge had paid attention to the interests of the workers. Moreover, complete tyranny and pursuit of self-interest were likely as long as workers were so dependent on the goodwill of their employers. The amazing growth in production astounded even many contemporaries. Indeed, Hugo befittingly portrays this astonishment: Father Madeleine became immensely wealthy despite investing in the community.

According to the historian Eric J. Hobsbawm, a significant 'take-off' took place primarily in the 1780s, enabling a seemingly continuous, fast and unlimited increase of people, goods and services.[9] From that moment, a steadily accelerating development commenced, characterized by faith in continuous growth and expansion. In its initial stages, this development came about so quickly that the social order could not accommodate the changes. Differing from Victor Hugo's idealized picture, employees were made a passive part of the industrial machine. Labour did not need to be skilled. It was often poorly trained and disorganized. At the same time, the state refused to intervene in the determination of wages and – in the spirit of liberalism – permitted employers to decide matters to their own advantage. For this reason the social effects of industrialism were local. In Hugo's imaginary Montreuil-sur-Mer things could well be cosy while the situation in an adjacent town might be completely different. In England, association – and with it the cooperation of the workers – was banned by law in 1799, by the so-called Combination Act, apparently due to fears brought on by the revolution in France.[10]

Workers could not get their rights recognized through legislation and counter-reactions appeared among workers in the new industrial jobs as well as those in more traditional occupations. Workers became aware of the means at their disposal. They could protest through strikes and, in extreme cases, by destroying the employers' property. These means had been actively used by workers during the eighteenth century – albeit with varying success. In western England, for example, feelings became heated in the 1720s among textile workers. When weavers' demands were not met, they broke into the houses of their masters, destroying wool and breaking looms. Similar 'negotiations' took place in the mining industry. In the 1740s, the miners of the Northumberland coalfields rioted, burning machines and finally managing to secure a pay rise. Machinery was destroyed and coal was burned in the riots of 1765 as well; these resulted in miners gaining the right to choose their employer at the end of their annual contracts.[11]

The destruction of machinery was thus used as a means to pressure employers, although such a method could not lead far in contract negotiations. Violence was directed more at the machinery than the employers. The new technology, especially the 'work-saving machinery', was seen as a satanic threat that had to be forcefully countered. James Hargreaves, the pioneer of spinning technology, was the first to experience the magnitude of this fear. When Hargreaves began using his Spinning Jenny looms in 1768, the employees quickly realized that the new machine would reduce the manpower needed to one tenth of what it had been. Thus the workers broke into the factory at night to destroy the apparatus. Hargreaves was forced to begin again. He moved to Nottingham and established a new textile mill. He had, however, spent a great deal of his capital. Hargreaves was penniless when he died in 1778, despite the fact that looms had spread throughout England during the intervening ten-year period.[12]

Luddism, the more systematic destruction of machines, reached its peak in 1811–13. Luddism is usually taken to have begun in December 1811 when employers started to receive mysterious threatening letters from a person called Ned Ludd. Contemporaries associated the threats with the wave of loom-breaking that erupted at the same time. As early as December 1811, *The Nottingham Review* called the culprits 'Luddites'.[13] When machine-breaking became a mass phenomenon, Great Britain had already long been at war with France and drifted into a severe economic recession.[14] A central factor contributing to the rise of Luddism has been seen to lie in the conflict between the economic crisis and the mechanization of industry. At the time, economic planning had no holistic view that would have helped through the crisis. Industrialists imagined they could improve their situation by making major investments in the new technology and thus cutting labour costs.[15] Thus Luddism may be seen as a reminder that the employer-side had gone too far in thinking of the workforce as simply a passive factor in production.

It needs to be kept in mind, however, that work in industrial society was significantly different from that of pre-industrial times. In the pre-industrial community production units were families, where a great variety of tasks were carried out, land was cultivated and handicrafts were made. Industrial society left factory workers with no source of income other than their cash salaries. The workers who had crammed into the cities and industrial estates no longer produced their own food and were thus at their employers' mercy.[16] It is thus no surprise that the severe plight of the winter of 1811–12 was first felt by the factory workers.

The aim of the Luddites was clearly to prevent the introduction of new labour-saving machines, especially in the textile industry. The government took strong action, however. Capital punishment was decreed for the breaking of machinery and the army was sent against the Luddites. By 1816 all opposition had been completely stamped out.[17]

In its initial stages the Industrial Revolution developed extremely rapidly and no group in society was willing to slow down the process. Even Luddism – which never became more than an expression of fear and desperation – was powerless to slow things down. Attacks on machinery and their inventors lost meaning as soon as inventions ceased to be the result of random activity. Towards the beginning of the nineteenth century technological innovation was the result of systematic work, and thus became difficult to resist simply through the destruction of machinery.

From the start, industrialization was tied to urban culture. Workers were enticed to these densely populated urban areas in great numbers. This development is represented well by the fact that in 1750 Britain had two cities with a population of over 50,000, London and Edinburgh, yet in 1801 there were already eight such cities and in 1851 as many as twenty-nine, nine of which had a population exceeding 100,000. In 1851 the majority of the British already lived in cities.[18] During the first half of the nineteenth century conditions in urban areas became miserable and dissatisfaction was demonstrated through riots and protests. It was a long time, however, before the workers' grievances were addressed. The Combination Act of 1799 was repealed in 1824. A central national organization of trade unions and federations was established in 1834.[19] Its membership rose to half a million almost immediately, well demonstrating the need for a representative organ as well as the high expectations people had of it. The industrialist Robert Owen became especially recognized as a spokesman for the workers, aspiring to arrange the workers' working and living conditions in an exemplary manner – perhaps he was the role model for Hugo's Father Madeleine. He put into effect a ten-hour working day, for example, something that was only achieved through legislation as late as 1847.[20] In the year following this, Karl Marx and Friedrich Engels published *The Communist Manifesto*, a work that had a profound impact on views about the future of industrial, capitalist society.

Industrialization also brought about a redefinition of the workers' cultural identity. The working people in the cities had distanced themselves from the popular culture of the countryside, thus providing fertile ground for new forms of culture. Various visual attractions from peek cupboards to magic lantern presentations became popular in nineteenth-century cities, clearing the way for modern popular culture. When the social consciousness of the working people awakened, a class-conscious workers' culture also took form, appearing as thriving literary and theatrical activities as well as new song traditions and sports. In practice, this kind of cultural consciousness did not become strong until the end of the century as it required the overall organization of the working class. At the same time, social consciousness was to find theoretical possibilities as Karl Marx's (1818–83) three-volume work *Capital* (*Das Kapital*, 1867–94) excited European thought. These ideological and theoretical changes came about with a delay, however, which lasted throughout the century.

The environmental problems of the industrial centres emerged much sooner than these cultural changes. Water and sewage services were lacking, the air was polluted and a heavy dust continually hung over cities like Manchester and Leeds. On top of all this, cholera epidemics and sexually transmitted diseases spread at an explosive rate. The poet William Wordsworth (1770–1850) described the bleak appearance of the industrial city in his 1814 poem 'The Excursion':

> Meanwhile, at social Industry's command,
> How quick, how vast an increase! From the germ
> Of some poor hamlet, rapidly produced
> Here a huge town, continuous and compact,
> Hiding the face of earth for leagues – and there,
> Where not a habitation stood before,
> Abodes of men irregularly massed
> Like trees in forests, – spread through spacious tracts.
> O'er which the smoke of unremitting fires
> Hangs permanent, and plentiful as wreaths
> Of vapour glittering in the morning sun.[21]

On visiting Manchester, the French liberal Alexis de Tocqueville indeed commented: 'Civilization works its miracles, and civilized man is turned back almost into a savage.'[22] Focusing on maximizing profits, early industrialists were not particularly interested in improving conditions for their workers. The experience of the pioneering countries of industrialization served as a warning example for those that followed. In Finland, for example, it was noted with concern in 1857 that 'the condition of the worker is becoming . . . as wretched as in industry-proud England'.[23]

In the English literature of the time, numerous descriptions of misery in the cities can be found. These depictions were social commentary that shocked contemporaries. The best-known fictional industrial centre is perhaps Charles Dickens's Coketown in the novel *Hard Times* (1854). In the book, Dickens describes a town that consists of endless rows of houses, cobblestone streets and canals. No fountains, squares, parks or even churches are to be found.

> It was a town of red brick, or of brick that would have been red if the smoke and ashes had allowed it; but, as matters stood it was a town of unnatural red and black like the painted face of a savage. It was a town of machinery and tall chimneys, out of which interminable serpents of smoke trailed themselves for ever and ever, and never got uncoiled. It had a black canal in it, and a river that ran purple with illsmelling dye, and vast piles of building full of windows where there was a rattling and a trembling all day long, and where the piston of the steamengine worked monotonously up and down, like the head of an elephant in a state of melancholy madness. It contained several large streets all very like one another, and many small streets still more like one another, inhabited by people equally like one another, who all went in and out at the same hours, with the same sound upon the same pavements, to do the same work, and to whom every day was the same as yesterday and tomorrow, and every year the counterpart of the last and the next.[24]

The novel focuses on a harsh, unimaginative father who realizes only too late that he has brought his children up to become cynical citizens of industrial society. In the industrial centre Dickens portrays, the residents have come to resemble their surroundings; they are akin to standardized machine parts, operating like automatons from day to day. From the city itself, everything imaginative or attractive has been lost or removed as unnecessary. Coketown is a nightmare vision, not a realistic reflection of contemporary reality. Yet it is distantly reminiscent of the smoke-covered, foul-smelling industrial cities that were born around the world: Manchester, Leeds and Birmingham in the British Isles, Merseburg and Essen in Germany, and Lille in France.[25]

In England, France and Germany, the first half of the nineteenth century may be called a period of abjectification. Change only began to take place in the mid-nineteenth century, partly as a result of the increased participation of the workers. The fact that the new technology had had time to spread to new spheres of life and embrace the entire society was also significant. At the same time, awareness of its consequences unavoidably increased. Machines contained a destructive power, one that could appear in sudden catastrophes or spread gradually, especially in the cities, the cauldron of steam technology.

At the start of the nineteenth century, technology was still viewed either in a romantic or a utilitarian way. The utilitarians believed in science and innovation, profit and power, machines and progress, money and increased ease and comfort. They believed that these values would spread merely through free trade. The Romantics, on the other hand, offered an alternative to this faith in rationality, emphasizing the past, the countryside and lost values. According to the historian Lewis Mumford, Romanticism was a regressive movement, lacking a real objective: Romanticism was 'an escapist movement'.[26] Thus Mumford sees Romanticism as an ideology related to industrialization. Romanticism has often been described as the 'age of emotion', critical of the Enlightenment culture and devotion to rationality of the preceding century. In Mumford's interpretation, the rationality that was criticized was not, however, that of the Enlightenment ideology but the contemporary industrial-technological attitude that was so much closer to home for the Romantics.

In his *Victorians and the Machine* (1968), Herbert L. Sussman has attempted to analyse the relationship of nineteenth-century English authors to the new technology. Literary authors were generally Romantics rather than utilitarians. They were Romantics to the extent that they practically ignored the achievements of steam technology and located their fictions in a time preceding these inventions.[27] William Morris turned this principle into an actual rule in his essay *The Earthly Paradise*:

> Forget six counties overhung with smoke,
> Forget the snorting steam and piston stroke,

Forget the spreading of the hideous town;
Think rather of the pack-horse on the down,
And dream of London, small and white and clean . . .[28]

It is interesting that many fierce opponents of technology were aristocrats, whether in England, France or the southern states of the United States. *Laissez-faire* agreed splendidly with bourgeois ideology: thus open opposition was to be found among the aristocracy. This should not, however, be understood too unconditionally. In an essay for a writing competition for the Academy of Dijon in 1750, the author of the French Enlightenment, Jean Jacques Rousseau, already argued that technological advances were nothing but harmful to humankind. In Germany, Friedrich Schiller took the machine as an example of the decay of contemporary culture in his *Über die ästhetische Erziehung des Menschen in einer Reihe von Briefen* (1795): machinery's 'monotonous sound of constantly turning wheels' exemplified the whole of modern culture.[29]

In England, the cradle of the Industrial Revolution, numerous opponents of technological advances could be found among artistic and literary circles. One such pessimist was the poet and artist William Blake (1757–1827). England was at war for thirty-five of the seventy years he lived. At the time, wars were becoming ever more total and increasingly international. With significant technological changes taking place at the same time, the world seemed to be turning inhumane and mechanistic. The two targets of Blake's wrath were inhumane machinery and war. Often he went as far as to connect technology and war, since better technical skills helped forge better swords and to cast larger cannons. Together they formed a 'loud sounding hammer of destruction'.[30]

In reality, Blake's knowledge of the new technology was limited. He lived in London, whereas most modern industry was in the north. In his entire life, Blake never travelled north of London and thus based his views mainly on hearsay and the press. His poems include water-wheels long after the advent of steam technology. But he created a credible vision of the advancement of technology that many found convincing. Influential it was not, since Blake's poetry was little known at the time.

Blake's rage against the machine reflects well, however, the general sentiments of the era of machine-breaking towards the strange and fearsome innovations. In his poems, the machine is linked with the irrational and satanic. Often he juxtaposes the modern, chaotic culture of machinery with religion and its goal of harmony and peace:

> I turn my eyes to the Schools & Universities of Europe
> And there behold the Loom of Locke, whose Woof rages dire,
> Wash'd by the Water-wheels by Newton: black the cloth
> In heavy wreathes folds over every Nation: cruel Works
> Of many Wheels I view, wheel without wheel, with cogs tyrannic
> Moving by compulsion each other, not as those in Eden, which,
> Wheel within Wheel, in freedom revolve in harmony & peace.[31]

In this poem Blake sees the machine as representative of the entire mechanistic worldview, strongly shaped by John Locke and Isaac Newton. The problems of industrialization were thus indirectly the result of philosophy and empirical physical sciences.

William Blake participated in the debate concerning industrialization through his art. He did not aspire to play an active role in decision-making. When it came to concrete action, a more significant representative of literary circles was Lord George Byron (1788–1824) who, according to an encyclopaedia description, was 'an adventurous and disappointed aristocrat, a poet with an understanding of nature's wild beauty, a high-handed, self-pitying exile, a sensitive lover and reckless freedom fighter'.[32] Byron studied at Cambridge and there wrote his first collection of poems, *Hours of Idleness* (1807). From 1809 to 1811 he travelled in southern Europe and returned to England only a little before the outbreak of Luddism. From 1811 to 1816 he participated actively in politics as a representative of the House of Lords. In 1816 he moved to Switzerland, never to return to England. He lived in Italy and, in the end, participated in the Greek War of Independence.

The most realistic period in Byron's work is characterized by the travel account *Childe Harold*, published in 1812. It is generally felt that difficult social conditions and the dismal fate of the workers is reflected in the cynical tone of the work. Lord Byron was, in fact, one of the few members of parliament who showed any compassion for the Luddites. When the law against the breaking of machines was passed by parliament in 1812, Byron failed to receive support from representatives either in the Lords or the Commons despite his masterful rhetoric.[33]

In a session of parliament on 25 February 1812, the first speech was given by Lord Holland, to whom Byron replied. This famous speech has become almost clichéd:

> In the foolishness of their hearts, they imagined that the maintenance and well-doing of the industrious poor were objects of greater consequence than the enrichment of a few individuals by any improvement – in the implements of trade – which threw the workmen out of employment, and rendered the labourer unworthy of his hire. And it must be confessed that although the adoption of the enlarged machinery in that state of our commerce which the country once boasted might have been beneficial to the master without being detrimental to the servant; yet, in the present situation of our manufactures, rotting in warehouses, without a prospect of exportation, with the demand for work and workmen equally diminished, frames of this description tend materially to aggravate the distress and discontent of the disappointed sufferers.[34]

Despite this moving and impressive speech, Byron received no support. The Frame Breaking Bill was passed, with capital punishment as the maximum penalty for offenders. The Romantic yearning for the pastoral idyll of a pre-technological past had no influence on political decision-making yet it continued to affect people's everyday thoughts and feelings.

In the course of the nineteenth century, industrialization and technology unavoidably penetrated new areas of life. At the same time, people became more aware that development could, from the very first, have taken a different course. The ultimate in oppositional fantasies can be said to be Samuel Butler's novel of 1872, the satirical utopia *Erewhon, or Over the Range*. The events are situated in an imaginary country where people have renounced machines and where even the bearing of a watch is a criminal offence.[35] In this utopian novel, technology has driven humanity to a crisis that can be averted only through destroying all machines. Butler's message is a 'complete annihilation of machinery': 'we should destroy as many of them as we can possibly dispense with, lest they should tyrannize over us even more completely'.[36] The breaking of machines was not only an expression of existentialist fear but also a means of political influence.

Political awareness of the social and environmental changes was slow to come. The consequences of industrialization did, however, spur imaginations, producing both fantastic visions of the future and dystopian nightmares. The French anarchist P. J. Proudhon envisioned a situation in which urban dwellers came to yearn for the countryside when it no longer existed. They had awoken too late. In Proudhon's pessimistic vision, the countryside has been destroyed. Supporters of private property have divided the country into little pens. On top of this, the revolution in transportation has strewn the open landscape with roads and a network of railways.[37]

In western Europe, environmental changes were observed in the industrial centres early on, yet realization came as quickly in the colonized peripheries of Europe that had been subjects to exploitative economy. The Scandinavian countries, especially Norway and Finland, produced raw materials. The rich forests of the north were recklessly shorn with little thought of the future. By the middle of the century it was already clear that the exploitation of natural resources could not continue without grave consequences. It was finally decided that the forest could be taxed only in proportion to its capacity for renewal. The Finnish author Zachris Topelius's poem 'Deforestation' ('Metsänhaaskaus') from 1874 speaks of the fear of modernization and the disastrous effects of industrialization:

> They strip and sell thee, my country!
> They take away thine warm winter fleece
> like drunkards, they trade every mother's best coat,
> for a drop of spirit.
> Thou were already poor even with your treasures;
> true that earlier thine beautiful, proud pines,
> those sturdy northern lads
> clothed in the darkest of green, used to rot for no reason;
> true that the ploughman's axe
> brought light and air to the wilderness,

brought freedom, justice, and bread,
cleared the road for western learning;
but today's cruel axe sweeps everything
like an angel of death and clears
the swamps, moors, valleys, fields and ridges,
pitilessly attacks the old man and the child,
both the youth on the hill in its spring dress
and the oldster with its beard of moss.[38]

'Today's cruel axe', mentioned by Topelius, is a critical characterization of the industrial-technical culture that was seen to threaten the traditional, centuries-old way of life in which nature and people had lived in harmony. Naturally, the picture was a Romantic idealization, yet the compounded impact of industrialism was blatantly obvious especially in the last decades of the nineteenth century. In Finland, the protection of forests had, however, begun early on. One of the most popular natural attractions, the scenic ridge of Punkaharju, became state-owned as early as 1840 and its landscape has since been protected.

In the end-of-the-century environmental thinking nature and culture were thought of as a unified whole. Both were threatened by industrial society. Ernst Rudorff, a leading figure in the German movement emphasizing locality and regional particularities, painted a distressing picture of the end-result of the industrial age in his book *Heimatschutz* (1901):

What have the past decades done to the world and especially to Germany? What has become of our beautiful, beloved home district with its picturesque mountains, rivers, castles and old towns. . . . The perspective of a single individual is infinitely small compared with that of the huge fatherland; the more horrendous, then, for him who keeps his eyes open, to see the changes in this small area, indicating a diversity of destruction. On the one hand, the exploitation by the various industrial establishments of all natural power and treasures, the devastation of the landscape by power lines, railways, the wood industry . . . for material gain alone . . . ; on the other, speculation with tourism, the repulsive praise of scenic beauty and simultaneous obliteration of all things original, of these particulars that make nature nature.[39]

At least in its initial stages, industrialization meant exactly the kind of exploitation described by Rudorff: it was exploitative or plunder economy, *Raubwirtschaft*, that paid no mind to diminishing natural resources. The 'picturesque home district' was ravaged by industrial establishments, railways and power lines. The ideal encompassed not only original, untouched nature but also cultural inheritance with its 'castles and old towns'. From this fusion of nature and culture was born the ideal of the home district, the *Heimat*, that should be protected against the onslaught of modernization. As the later chapters of this book will show, the victims of plunder were not only the home districts and European peripheries but also other continents. Colonialism had an essential role in the history of European industrialization.

As may be seen from the preceding investigation, the effects of industrialization were not only material and physical but also spiritual. Industry and technology fed the imagination: on one hand they inspired wishfully nostalgic conceptions of the past, of times lost, on the other hand they generated expectations regarding the future that I shall return to at the end of the book. The cultural effects of industrialization pose, however, a much more far-reaching question – so extensive, in fact, that the process is difficult to conceive of at all in its full complexity. Industrialization was also linked to a philosophy, a faith in duplication and its applicability in all areas of life. Before long, the most varied cultural products came to be included in industrial activity, and material products were accompanied by more abstract phenomena – even time and space, for example – as the significance of distances changed with innovations in transportation.

2

The Faustian Man: A Society in Motion

Johann Wolfgang von Goethe's (1749–1832) lyric play *Faust* (1808) begins with a scene where the main character sits anxiously at his desk in what is described as a 'high-vaulted, narrow Gothic chamber'. Faust is 'a Master, even Doctor too' in possession of knowledge, and poses a challenge to the bounds of propriety:

> True, I am more clever than all the vain creatures,
> The Doctors and Masters, Writers and Preachers;
> No doubts plague me, nor scruples as well.
> I'm not afraid of devil or hell.[1]

With all his knowledge, Faust is above mundane matters and has no respect for the gods or fear of the infernal flames. Despite his knowledge, everything seems futile to him, however, because book learning has brought no material benefits: 'Nor have I gold or things of worth, Or honours, splendours of the earth.' Finally, Faust strikes a bargain with the devil and reacquires his youth. At the same time, he aspires to add to his material well-being.

Historians have often presented *Faust* as exemplary of the modern person. Western people are determined by a thirst for knowledge similar to that of Goethe's hero, who shirks from nothing to increase his knowledge. Goethe's work displays a mistrust towards religion; true knowledge is not something that can be found in holy texts, and Faust's passion for knowledge involves a practical denial of his religious beliefs. Despite critiques of religion throughout the eighteenth century, the Great Revolution in France shook the foundations of the Catholic Church. Authors like Chateaubriand experienced this as a catastrophe; indeed, in his *Génie du christianisme*, he tried to re-establish an appreciation of Catholic beliefs. Religion came to symbolize a stable world that could not be reconciled with the dynamism of post-revolutionary society.

The French author Stendhal (the pen name of Marie-Henri Beyle; 1783–1842) described contemporary social life in an ironic manner in his novel *The Red and the Black* (*Le rouge et le noir*, 1830), in which the young Julien Sorel tries to find his place on the social ladder, first by joining the army and later by becoming a priest. The novel is a sweeping portrait of early nineteenth-century France and its different social thoughts and sensibilities. Sorel is interested in the Church only because of his attempt to rise above his rural background. When Julien has to enter the seminary, this is described as an entry into a nightmare:

> From a distance he saw the gilt cross over the door. He walked towards it slowly, feeling as if his knees would give way. 'There is that hell on earth which I shall never leave!' After some time he summoned enough courage to ring the bell; the sound of the bell reverberated within, as in a sepulchre. He waited ten minutes before a pale man, in black, came to open the door. Julien looked at him, but was forced to turn his eyes away, the doorkeeper's face was so terrifying. His greenish, flashing eyes roamed like a cat's; his immovable eyelids suggested not a trace of feeling; and over his protruding teeth opened thin, harsh lips. Yet that face did not betray any inherent cruelty, but rather that complete insensibility in which Julien read that whatever he might say would be received with indifference and contempt.[2]

Stendhal's description can be interpreted as an expression of the anti-clerical sentiments of the Restoration period in France in 1815–1830. On the one hand, the Great Revolution had meant a

transfer of sacral rituals on to political and social life, best epito-
mized by the festivals and rites of the 1789 Revolution. On
the other hand, a marked popular anti-clericalism arose during the
decades following the revolution, both in the cities and in the
countryside, protesting religious revival and the conservative
longing for a strengthening of the Catholic Church.[3] Although it
is clear that the mobile society created by the great changes in
society diminished the role of religion in Faust's realm, the scholarly world and the world of science, it is just as obvious that new
popular forms of religion appeared during the first decades of the
century, especially in the Protestant areas, where revivalism and a
'new awakening' stressed a simple, personal relationship with God.
In the 1820s, the Plymouth Brethren movement, for example,
claimed that the Church had abandoned many of its basic truths.
Many other revivalist movements also became popular, and it can
be argued that as industrialization started to spread through Europe
there was an ever-growing interest in the inner lives and transcendental experiences of human beings. Despite the fact that these
religious tendencies underlined the importance of the immaterial,
stable world, the nineteenth century is characterized by material
values and ambition, and this dichotomy can already be seen in
Goethe's *Faust*.

From our present-day perspective, *Faust* is of interest to us
because its main character uses his newfound position to achieve
material comfort; it is almost as if material prosperity were the
highest objective of learning. Goethe's *Faust* symbolizes, then, the
insatiable thirst for advancement felt by the modern person while
also telling a story of the constant pursuit of material well-being.
Both of these elements were undoubtedly strongly present in
nineteenth-century European culture. In the aftermath of the
Industrial Revolution faith in the inventiveness of humans was
perhaps stronger than ever before. At the same time, entrepre-
neurship was in its golden age and industrial culture seemed to
know no limits. The Faustian man can be seen in a more abstract
fashion, however: it exemplifies the continuous longing for knowledge experienced by people in the west and their desire to move
ever forward. Movement is natural to them, as is discontent with
what has already been achieved. It is clear, of course, that 'people'

is not a neutral category here, and the Faustian man is a gendered concept. In Goethe's work the thirst for knowledge is represented as a male feature and in the storyline the yearning for economic power is closely linked with expanding masculine domination. Knowing how important female agency was in religious movements and organizations and how excluded women were from the world of science, it seems that the tension between economic and scientific progress and the religious worldview reveals a gender gap in nineteenth-century Europe.[4]

The nineteenth century may be termed a century of progress – at least in the sense that faith in progress had no rival in European public sentiment and politics. Of course, there were pessimists who criticized the rosier visions but their voices gained strength only towards the end of the century. The whole gloomy view of the decline of western culture during the *fin de siècle* period can well be seen as a counter-reaction to the optimism that had ruled the early stages of industrial culture. As Friedrich Engels said, history always has its winners and its losers, yet general sentiments in the early nineteenth century afforded the losers' voices no platform. In 1893, Engels wrote: 'History is about the most cruel of all goddesses, and she leads her triumphal car over heaps of corpses, not only in war, but also in "peaceful" economic development.'[5] In Engels's description it is history that holds the reins: movement is essential although someone always falls under the wheels, even when social development seems, to all accounts, peaceful, and the economy prospers.

The Luddites desperately attempted to stop the 'triumphal car', the onward march of the Faustian man, but with little result. Authors like William Blake could remind people of the 'satanic mills', but their critical voices were discovered only later. Thinking of nineteenth-century counter-culture, one is particularly reminded of the musical dramatist Richard Wagner's opera tetralogy, *The Ring of the Nibelung*, the first drafts for which were created at the end of the 1840s but which only premiered at the first opera festival in Bayreuth in 1876. In the introductory drama of the series, *The Rhinegold*, the target for criticism is particularly the scheming aristocracy, represented in the piece by the gods inhabiting Valhalla. The tetralogy revolves around a ring that allows its owner to rule the world, which is pursued by dwarves and giants as well as the gods. Wagner clearly attributes working-class characteristics to both dwarves and giants. In the last opera, *The Twilight of the Gods*, avarice leads to the inevitable collapse of the entire world order. Lust for money and power has no future without love and compassion.[6] Familiar with the rise of industrialism and the continually increasing importance of money and the economy, many of Wagner's contemporaries could undoubtedly recognize the criticism that he hid in his operas.

The central role of the belief in progress in nineteenth-century European thought was especially apparent in one area: transportation. As economic activity increased it became ever more important to move information and goods faster than before. The growing – and indeed greatly increased – dynamism also attracted the attention of contemporaries. As the Finnish printer K. E. Eurén commented in his 1863 work *Steam Engines: Their Invention and Practice*: 'Steam has caused an unpredictable change among the people and in their peaceful lives, enlivening movement among them and strengthening the numerous ties they had been almost unaware of in the past.'[7] Although Eurén emphasizes the significance of steam technology in the forming of 'numerous ties' and in increasing mobility, the change was not simply a matter of transformation in the capacity for physical transportation: images and conceptions were also capable of spreading faster than ever before.

Naturally, the spread of the Industrial Revolution was closely connected with developments in transport technology. The limitations imposed by the use of the waterways and horse-power on the expansion of production and extension of markets became obvious quite early on. The channels were frozen in the winter and horse-powered transport depended on food production. In addition, transportation with horses was also subject to changes in the weather. The spread of industrial production called for a more efficient and reliable transport system. It was no surprise, then, that steam technology came to be applied to transportation as well.

The first application of steam was the steamboat, the building and use of which spread quickly throughout Europe. The spreading of the steamboat did not demand as extensive structural changes in the transportation network as did the train somewhat later. The first steamboats were in use already in the eighteenth century. In 1788 the Scottish banker Patrick Miller produced a steam-powered paddlewheeler in cooperation with the engineer William Symington. Mechanically powered transoceanic transportation did not, however, begin until the next century. The American frigate the *Savannah* was equipped with a steam engine in 1819 and steam-powered ships were to be found chugging along as far as the Mediterranean and the Baltic Sea only a decade later.[8]

The train was born by simply placing the steam-hauled carriages on rails. In 1804, Richard Trevithick (1771–1833) built a 10-ton locomotive for a track that ran from the Pen-y-Darren Iron Works to the Glamorganshire canal. It was able to pull five carriages and carry seventy people. Its travelling speed was 5 miles per hour. In the beginning, the practical significance of the invention was slight, and Trevithick thus decided to use the device for entertaining the public. In 1808, he built his first passenger train, which he displayed in a show called 'Catch-Me-Who-Can'. The train went round a circular track inside a fencing and the audience could pay to ride around in carriages pulled by the locomotive. Initially, the train was only a technical curiosity – similar to movies at the end of the century.[9]

In the early years of the nineteenth century, there was great enthusiasm for the new application. The moving machine captivated the public. Placed on wheels, the steam engine did not awaken the same frantic fear as steam engines in factories, and nothing akin to Luddism arose against trains. It seems that this was so because the social impact of trains was not equally immediate. In addition, there was a practical need for the train in England due to the war against France and the resulting lack of horses on the home front. The situation was thus awkward in two ways. Accelerating industrial production required better mobility, yet at the same time the war had caused existing transport to deteriorate. For this reason, the steam locomotive quickly found new developers. The best known of these were George Stephenson (1781–1848) and his son Robert (1803–59). As early as 1814, George Stephenson built an experimental locomotive named *My Lord*. His second engine was *Blücher*, named probably after the famous Prussian general following Napoleon's final defeat at Waterloo in

June 1815. It is possible that Stephenson only renamed his earlier engine after the battle. It remains clear however that *Blücher* became a success, and Stephenson used it for collecting money in a train exhibition near Waterloo in London. It is as clear that it was the famous *Rocket* – a locomotive designed jointly by George and Robert Stephenson and completed in 1829 – that marked the move in the direction of railway transportation.[10] The final breakthrough came in the following decade, when railway tracks were laid in the United States (1830), Belgium and Germany (1835), France (1837), and also in Russia (1838).

Application of the new technology was swift, and decisions were made with little thought to the kind of future chosen in making them. Progress was so fast, that already in the 1830s nostalgia for the 'quiet life' of the past was beginning to appear in public sentiment. The railway brought punctuality and speed but seemed impersonal. In his book *English Pleasure Carriages*, published in 1837, William Bridges Adams wrote:

In the first place, steam is a mere labourer – a drudge who performs his work without speech or sign, with dogged perseverance but without emotion. By dint of the garb in which he is clad, the machine which serves him for a body, he sometimes puts on the appearance of a live thing, shaking his polished metal clothing like an armoured knight: but this is only when he is stationary. His travelling grab is rough and rude, his breath is sulphureous, his voice is hissing, his joints creak, the anointing of his limbs gives forth an unpleasing gaseous odour, he carries with him a kitchen and a fuel chamber, and his whole appearance is black and unsightly. He may be personified when speaking *of* him; but no one pats his neck or speaks *to* him in a voice of encouragement. It is not so with a horse or horses. They are beautiful and intelligent animals, powerful yet docile; creatures that respond to kindness, and shrink from cruelty and injustice. The driver and owner can love them or feel proud of them; they step with grace, and can vary their form and movements in a thousand ways. They are creatures of individual impulses.[11]

Even though industrialization and the steam engine rapidly increased awareness of the modern machine culture in the early nineteenth century, the most significant pioneer of the new culture was the train – which in the United States, for example, became a national obsession in the 1830s. The iron horse became the embodiment of the age: an instrument of power, speed, noise, fire, iron and smoke. At the same time, it came to be a symbol of the human ability to overcome obstacles set by nature. Commenting on Alexis de Tocqueville's *Democracy in America* in 1840 in the *Edinburgh Review,* John Stuart Mill called the locomotive a perfect symbol that required no external meanings: its physical attributes being enough in themselves. Seeing the efficient machine in the terrain makes one immediately understand the superiority of the present over the past.[12] Technology was seen to reflect the power of humans over nature. The superior effect of the railway was described in the following way in 1844:

> Steam disposes space . . . Travelling has changed from a lonely pil-grimage to a triumphal cortege . . . The caravans of travellers twist across the known world as if moving on the wind. Here, they cross ploughed fields on their iron rails, there, they climb and descend hills, leaving a trail of foam behind them like the carriage of the god of the sea.[13]

In the United States, the train came to symbolize national unity, particularly in the 1850s and 1860s. The railway extending from the East Coast to the West Coast was seen as a lifeline, transform-ing a heterogeneous nation into a unified whole. The railway had a similar integrating significance in Russia, where the first 27 kilo-metre-long track was built between St Petersburg and the Czar's Summer Palace in 1838. The real boom in construction came, however, in the mid-1840s, when tracks were laid in the direction of both Moscow and Prussia. The press celebrated the first railroad 'as the triumph of culture and progress'.[14] With the passing of the nineteenth century, the train provided the setting for numerous newspaper columns and short stories in the press.[15]

It is clear that the train was greeted in different ways by different classes. The mercantile population saw the train as providing new possibilities for trade. The farmers and cattle breeders opposed the railways that pushed their way through grazing land, probably killing livestock. The mere laying of the tracks was an intricate operation, dividing opinion. Most often the construction development was hardest on those who had the least to gain from it. In Finland, for example, the author K. A. Tavaststjerna described the building of the Riihimäki–St Petersburg track and the life of its victims in his novel *Hard Times* (*Hårda tider*) set in the famine of the 1860s. Tavaststjerna's attitude to change was clearly ambivalent because gains were achieved only at the expense of human suffering.[16]

The coming of the train has been splendidly described by the Finnish author Juhani Aho (1861–1921) in his novel *The Railway* (*Rautatie*, 1884). In some of his other writings Aho has also described technology and the feelings associated with it, in his short stories *When Father Brought Home the Lamp* (*Siihen aikaan, kun isä lampun osti*) and *The Clock* (*Kello*), both from 1884, for example. In the *Railway*, the main characters Matti and Liisa, who live far from the village in the backwoods of Korventausta, are almost the last to hear about the train on the whole of the Finnish peninsula. They are filled with many prejudices towards it, especially after Matti hears that the train is a horse that eats logs. Particularly interesting is the passage describing how Matti and Liisa contemplate the destructive power of the train.

And Liisa recounted how the dean's wife had told her that the railroad had run over a cow the past summer . . . and the cow had been split in two, one half of it on one side of the road . . .

– They say it doesn't look . . . just rides full gallop, even with a person in the way.

– Why be in the way?

– True, only a cow isn't fast enough . . . and it isn't clever . . .

– No, a person.

– They're not fast enough either . . . and people say they don't look . . . someone gets in their way . . . they only whistle and who doesn't quickly . . .

– Does it whistle?

– So they say . . .

– It keeps to its ways even in the country, you see.

– Then it's their own fault if they get in the way.

– Have to be mad, to get in the way, I suppose, when they could be walking somewhere else . . .

– Should stay away . . .

– They say it sometimes gets one from further off, if they're not far enough . . . one man was pulled in that'd gone too close . . . there's some attraction that pulls in like a rapid to its heart . . .

– And it just took him?

– I suppose.

– I think I'd have the heart to stand a bit further off, if ever I happened in the same country . . . I reckon I would.

– Reckon I would too.[17]

Juhani Aho describes the feelings of Matti and Liisa somewhat sarcastically. The new triumph of technology is greeted with great prejudice but with an attraction that they dare not admit. In the passage above, Matti and Liisa recount rumours they have heard of the destructive power of the train, yet they also assure each other of their fearlessness. Apparently the 'tremendous' speed of the train was in itself something that residents of remote villages simply could not imagine. 'The power that pulled one in' seemed mysterious and frightening. The mysteries of steam technology had not been revealed to the Finns living in the backwoods: 'But what on earth pulls this? That Matti could not understand . . .'[18]

It has often been said that early train travel included a thrilling attraction, that the pleasure brought by speed was combined with fear, because the passenger had surrendered himself to the mercy of technology. Feelings for the moving machine were conflicting. This conflict was affected essentially by the first train accidents, which made passengers aware of the dangers of such travel. 'Falling off the train' – that Matti and Liisa are so fearful of in the *Railway* – was not a real fear unlike the possibility of collision or derailment. The first serious train accident in Europe took place on 8 May 1842 when the local train between Paris and Versailles derailed due to the breakage of a locomotive axle and caught fire.[19] Quickly, a phenomenon known as the 'Railway Spine' came to be recognized. People who had experienced the accident began to fear the train and display symptoms of traumatic neurosis. Insurance companies were forced to consider whether such after-effects were sufficient

reason for compensation. As a consequence of this social phenomenon, physicians and psychologists took a stand on illnesses brought
on by the new technology. In the 1840s and the 1850s, the terms
'neurosis' and 'trauma' were still unknown concepts in medical
discourse. Rather, symptoms were interpreted pathologically or
pathoanatomically. When train neurosis was interpreted to result
from damage to the spinal cord caused by the physical shock on the
train, insurance was extended to cover it. It was not until the 1880s
that talk of the 'Railway Spine' was replaced with the idea of traumatic neurosis. Earlier, it had been primarily characterized by the
term 'shock', which signified the effects of accidents generally. The
concept referred mainly to physical rather than mental 'shocks'.[20]

The consequences of railway accidents were discussed in journals like *The Lancet* and *British Medical Journal* as well as in a number
of medical treatises in the 1860s.[21] Among the most influential
scholarly texts was John Eric Erichsen's work *On Railway and Other
Injuries of the Nervous System*, published in 1866. In Erichsen's book
we find a description of a typical sufferer of train neurosis:

> One of the most remarkable phenomena attendant upon this class of
> cases is, that at the time of the occurrence of the injury the sufferer is
> usually quite unconscious that any serious accident has happened to
> him. He feels that he has been violently jolted and shaken, he is perhaps
> somewhat giddy and confused, but he finds no bones broken, merely
> some superficial bruises or cuts on the head or legs, perhaps even no
> evidence whatever of external injury. He congratulates himself upon
> his escape from the imminent peril to which he has been exposed. He
> becomes unusually calm and self-possessed; assists his less-fortunate
> fellow sufferers, occupies himself perhaps actively in this way for several
> hours, and then proceeds on his journey. When he reaches his home,
> the effects of the injury that he has sustained begin to manifest them-
> selves. A revulsion takes place. He bursts into tears, becomes unusually
> talkative, and is excited. He cannot sleep, or, if he does, he wakes up
> suddenly with a vague sense of alarm.[22]

Erichsen's explanation was still based on pathology. During the train
accident, the nervous system of the victim had received an injury
that simply appeared in the form of psychological problems. In

1875, Erichsen published another book called *On Concussion of the Spine, Nervous Shock, and Other Obscure Injuries of the Nervous System, in their Medical and Medicolegal Aspects* in which his views have clearly taken a more psychopathological direction:

> It is important to observe that a serious accident may give rise to two distinct forms of nervous shock. . . . The first is mental or moral, and the second purely physical. These forms of 'shock' may be developed separately, or they may coexist. It is most important . . . to diagnose between these two, and if co-existing to assign to each other its proper importance.[23]

The more general move to a psychopathological approach did not occur until the 1880s when the concept of 'traumatic neurosis' was adopted.[24] It seems that the psychological complications caused by the train played a central role in the conceptualization of mental phenomena. It could even be argued that such speculation had an impact on psychoanalysis, as developed by Sigmund Freud. Catastrophes and traumatic experiences encouraged analysts to also search for 'biographical catastrophes' by which an individual's behaviour could be interpreted.

In his seminal work *The Railway Journey* (*Geschichte der Eisenbahnreise*, 1977) Wolfgang Schivelbusch analyses these developments and the mental reception of railway accidents. He does not however deal with the train neurosis as a gendered issue, even though, as Lynne Kirby has pointed out, the fear for an accident was an obvious form of 'male hysteria'. In contemporary medical discussion these psychological problems were not discussed explicitly as male questions. Instead, in the late nineteenth-century literature hysteria was often presented as a notably feminine feature.[25]

Schivelbusch argues that railway accidents in particular marked a mental turning point. This may be the case in western and central Europe, but steamship accidents were at least equally – if not even more – serious, often involving a greater number of casualties. In the Swedish, Russian and Finnish newspapers, there is almost no mention of train accidents in the 1840s and 1850s whereas a number of stories of steamer accidents can be found.[26] Reports of these accidents had become a part of the standard repertoire of the newspapers in the 1850s. Through news coverage, envisioning a catastrophe became common property. When, on 3 February 1853, the steamship *Parisien* was destroyed on the Rhône in France, the enormous explosion of the boiler that broke the ship into three parts and violently took the life of six people was reported as far as St Petersburg.[27] It is equally interesting that in 1842 the *Åbo Tidningar* extensively covered the fire aboard the *Lexington* on the Atlantic, yet did not even mention the train accident on the Paris–Versailles track. The destruction of the *Lexington* was described in detail: the fire was 'a terrible catastrophe, which caused the loss of several hundred lives'.[28]

Schivelbusch sees the train as the factor that carried industrialization over into the basic categories of perception, time and space. The earliest convention of describing the effects of train travel involved an account of the way in which it altered awareness of time and space. In its initial stages, the train made travel approximately three times faster than it had been during the period of horse-drawn carriages. The speed of the early English locomotives was between 20 and 30 miles an hour. When the railway line from Paris to Rouen and Orléans opened in 1843, the poet Heinrich Heine, who was living in Paris at the time, called it 'a gift from Providence', comparable to the invention of gunpowder or the printing press.[29] Heine's words clearly reflect the change in the perception of time and space brought about by the train:

> Even the elementary ideas of space and time are tottering; for by the railway space is annihilated, and only time remains. Oh, that we had money enough to kill the latter properly! In three hours and a half one can now go to Orleans, in the same time to Rouen. What will it be when the lines to Belgium and Germany shall be finished and connected with the railways of those countries? I seem to see the mountains and forests of every country coming to Paris. I smell the perfume of German lime-trees; the billows of the North Sea are bounding and roaring before my door.[30]

In addition to the experience of timelessness, the train also led to a more accurate and unified use of time. Greenwich Mean Time became the standard for the railway, first in England and, in the end, all over the world – especially after the dividing up of the globe into time zones according to Greenwich Mean Time at the International Meridian Conference in Washington in 1884.

The standardization of time speaks clearly of the powerful change that had taken place in transportation. It was necessary to create a means whereby increased movement could be controlled and coordinated. In addition to having an international significance due to spanning the separate countries of Europe, railways were also nationally important. Especially in the unification of Germany in the 1860s and the 1870s, the railways helped create cohesion in a politically fragmented area. Another characteristic feature of technical development in Europe was the way in which keeping up with new technology became a national issue: a nation had to demonstrate its ability not only in technological but also in artistic creativity.

3

From the Cult of Genius to Worship of Art

Significant changes in the conditions for creative activity took place in parallel with the industrial and technological revolution in the late eighteenth and early nineteenth centuries. At a time when industrial society was becoming ever more reliant on mass production, originality and individuality gained increasing emphasis in art: the age of reproduction appreciated inimitability. The question of civil rights and freedom of opinion and expression also determined the possibilities for artistic creation and presentation. At the beginning of the nineteenth century the press became increasingly influential as shaper of public opinion and as commentator of artistic phenomena.[1]

The end of the eighteenth century produced an artistic and ideological movement known as Romanticism. In our contemporary usage the words 'romantic' and 'romance' signify emotions and love, and 'romantics' are sometimes seen negatively as dreamers, detached from the world. At the time, however, Romanticism was interpreted differently. In the 1790s, the German philosopher Friedrich Schelling labelled the German literary and philosophical movement of the period Romanticism. Romanticism emphasized emotion, imagination, originality and freedom, and felt an affinity to nature, the mysteries of the human soul and the individual. Since then, thoughts, literature and art associated with Romanticism have been produced all over Europe. Many early Romantics were critical of social changes such as industrialization.

The eighteenth century had already seen an interest in emotional sensitivity, and this tradition was continued in the sensibility of the Romantics. The Romantics criticized the rigidity of Classicism, influenced by the aesthetics of antiquity, and yet did not reject antiquity – rather the interpretation of it changed.[2] Many Romantics thought that art should be given a central position in society, as had been the case in the city-states of ancient Greece. Where the Greeks had looked to their mythology for inspiration, newly born nations should examine their past and use their own folklore to the same effect. In this way, Romanticism nourished an emergent nationalism.

A good example of the interconnection and merging of Classicism and Romanticism is the novel *Atala* by François-René de Chateaubriand, which appeared in 1801. The author was an aristocrat who, caught in the upheavals of the French Revolution, was forced to flee to North America and England. Chateaubriand dreamt of writing a work to defend the significance of Christianity, to be entitled *Le Génie du christianisme* (*The Genius of Christianity*). *Atala* was meant to be the first part of this work but Chateaubriand published it separately. Following the spirit of eighteenth-century literature, the work was educative, emphasizing the Christian value of tolerance. It told the story of the tragic love between two young Indians, the Christian Atala and Chactas, a non-Christian belonging to a different tribe. Structurally the work resembles a Greek tragedy, where a fatal error arising from innocence or ignorance leads to inevitable catastrophe. Despite its classical precedents the novella became the first cult work of French Romanticism. Its lyrical descriptions of nature and its unrestrained emotional effusion impressed contemporaries and introduced something new. In the year of its appearance five printings of the book were made and it was promptly translated into Spanish, Italian, German and English. The cult piece was adapted for the theatre and images of the characters were popular on the walls of inns as well as homes.[3]

Atala immediately made Chateaubriand a central figure in literary publicity. At the same time it demonstrated the power literature wields, even politically. The book conveyed pessimism towards political unrest, and Chateaubriand was later to become an active supporter of 'conservatism': he was an aristocrat who had difficulty accepting the violence of the revolution and who would reminisce about the lost world of aristocracy with melancholy. In *Atala*, a sombre view of European culture is expressed by Father Aubrey, who attempts to comfort the dying Atala:

> Although you have lived in solitude, you have known sorrow; what would you have thought had you witnessed the evils of society, had your ears been assailed, as you set foot on Europe's shores, by the long cry of woe rising out of that ancient land? The hut dweller and the palace lord both suffer alike, and all lament together in this world. Queens have been seen weeping like simple women, and men have stood aghast at the volume of tears in the eyes of kings![4]

A characteristic feature of Romanticism was the belief in genius, in the creative individual, and after the appearance of *Atala* an effort was undoubtedly made to fit the mantle of genius also on the shoulders of the marginalized Chateaubriand. In 1790, the German philosopher Immanuel Kant had written that a genius was naturally endowed with the talent that gives the rule to art. Because innate creativity comes from nature it is nature – through genius – that determines the principles of art.[5] The admiration, and even the very cult, associated with genius was strongest in the sphere of music. Ludwig van Beethoven (1770–1827) became the symbol for creative genius, with his thick, ruffled hair as a sign of unconventional thinking and inexhaustible ideas.

In music, the admiration of individuality was most apparent in the success of virtuosos: their talents were seen as an expression of strictly personal endowments, and the virtuosos practically competed over who would go furthest in breaking with performance conventions. At the beginning of the nineteenth century the Genoan-born violinist Niccolò Paganini (1782–1840) was among the most sensational figures, bewildering his contemporaries with his virtuosity. Paganini made his debut in Milan in 1813 and became renowned in the musical centres of Paris, London and Vienna in subsequent decades.[6] His brilliant virtuosity led contemporaries to suspect that the artist had – like Goethe's Faust – struck a deal with the devil. In contemporary materials, diabolic descriptions of Paganini abound. In the 1830s, Heinrich Heine described the physiognomy and performance of the mysterious Italian maestro in his collection of short stories *Florentine Nights*. Constant references are made in the obsessive stories to death and necrophilic love, and Paganini is described as 'a dying gladiator', 'a corpse arisen from the grave' and 'a vampire with a violin'. Heine describes Paganini's appearance:

> At length there appeared upon the stage a dark form, which seemed to have arisen from the nether world. It was Paganini in his black dress-suit. The black dress-coat, and the black vest were of a horrid cut, such, perhaps, as is prescribed by infernal etiquette, at the court of Proserpine. The black trousers fluttered nervously about the thin legs. The long arms seemed increased in length by reason of the violin which he held in one hand, and the bow which he had in the other, and with which he almost touched the ground as he shook out his unprecedented bows before the audience. In the angular curves of his body lay a fearful woodenness, and at the same time something doltishly brutal, which must have excited a desire to laugh, had not his face, which appeared still more cadaverous in the blaze of the foot-lights, worn an expression so imploring, so stupidly submissive, that a horrible pity repressed our laughter.[7]

Paganini was simultaneously a comic and pitiful figure. Heine's text is a contemporary literary testimony, but even newspaper articles made reference to the artist's body, his distorted form, angular movements and his long, thin fingers, whose dance on the violin strings seemed supernatural.[8] No doubt Paganini intentionally created a diabolic image of himself: when outdoors, he used a dark overcoat that trailed the ground and – according to Heine – walked broadly, as if dragging 'iron fetters between his legs'.[9]

The publicity created by the newspapers and literature furthered the success of the virtuosos. In the public eye, Paganini's private life and musical career became intertwined to form an equally insepa-rable whole as did the true stories and rumours associated with him. In the 1830s another virtuoso entered onto the stage, the

Hungarian-born pianist Franz Liszt (1811–86) whose popularity grew to dimensions comparable to that accorded later to movie stars. Contemporaries were in fact hard put to understand what it was that made Liszt so fascinating. Explanations were sought even in natural phenomena such as magnetism and galvanism, of great popular interest at the time, with the idea that there were such natural forces in play in Liszt's persona that distinguished him from ordinary people – forces that could perhaps be understood but that were nevertheless unique. Liszt's magnetism also gave rise to suspicions concerning the unhealthy effects of the packed concert halls and salons: the lack of oxygen caused by the burning wax candles and the extreme closeness of the perspiring listeners caused music lovers to pass out.[10]

Paganini and Liszt were regarded as geniuses who did not simply follow learned conventions but changed the course of art. It is no coincidence that Paganini, Liszt and Beethoven were men: in the nineteenth century genius was first and foremost a male attribute.[11] At a time when women were seen as susceptible to the fantasy worlds created by novels and were presented as passive consumers of art, particularly of sentimental novels such as *Atala*, original, creative thinking was treated as a masculine characteristic.

When the Polish composer and pianist Frédéric Chopin was extolled as a creative genius his mistress George Sand, whose real name was Aurore Dupin (1804–76), was forced to hide behind a pseudonym in order to be taken seriously. Liszt's and Chopin's contemporaries included Clara Wieck (1819–96), the foremost female piano virtuoso of the time. She gave her first solo concert in 1830 at the age of eleven, first performing repertoires selected by her father Friedrich Wieck but later going on to more challenging works. After her marriage to Robert Schumann, she raised seven children, but never gave up performing and composing. Although publicity of the time was inclined to deny the existence of female genius, Robert Schumann gave expression to the difficulties female artists faced in their work as he revealingly noted in his diary in 1843: 'Clara has written a number of smaller pieces, which show a musicianship and a tenderness of invention such as she has never before attained. But children, and a husband who is always living in the realms of imagination, do not go well with composition. She cannot work at it regularly, and I am often disturbed to think how many tender ideas are lost because she cannot work them out.'[12]

It is of added interest that already in the eighteenth century women had played a significant role in the organization of collective creativity. The salons had offered opportunities for musical performances as well as literary discussions and learned debates. Many of the outstanding salons were presided over by women. An important base in Berlin had been the salon of Jewish-born Rahel Varnhagen (born Levin, 1771–1833), frequented by Schiller, Schlegel and Schleiermacher, among others.[13] While the importance of the salons diminished in the nineteenth century owing to an increase in public concerts and the literary publicity provided by the newspapers, the success of many artists like Chopin and Liszt, for example, was built on salon performances. The presence of these two cultures was obvious in the Mendelssohn family. Where Felix Mendelssohn Bartholdy (1809–47) successfully led his public concerts in the 1830s and the 1840s, his sister, the composer Fanny Hensel (1805–47) ran one of the most famous salons in Berlin, regularly organizing concerts.[14]

The rupture undergone in art in the nineteenth century can be examined not only in terms of the structural changes in publicity but also in terms of commercialism. The rise of the middle class emphasized the social significance of commerce, and thus art too became increasingly an object of exchange. The fate of Chateaubriand's memoirs, *Mémoires d'outre tombe*, is telling of the change in circumstances. He started writing his memoirs as early as the 1810s, with the intention of creating a panorama of the entire century. To be able to complete this major work the author had to sign a contract with a society of shareholders in 1836: he got an annual payment for the rest of his life, but in turn gave up the ownership of his *Mémoires*. Now he had the possibility of devoting himself to his writing in the last years of his life.[15] The work became a uniquely broad-ranging description of the time before and after the Great Revolution and appeared after the author's death in 1848.[16] To accomplish this, Chateaubriand could not help but plunge into the maelstrom of the new commercial culture.

It is obvious that after the French Revolution it became necessary to find new avenues for making art. Once the arts had become distanced from the service of the Church and princely courts, new opportunities for creative work had to be sought out. Chateaubriand's society of shareholders was an exceptional solution, as the majority of artists worked as private entrepreneurs. Travelling virtuosos themselves had to arrange venues for their concerts as well as hire any additional musicians they might need.

International virtuosos quickly learned to set a price on their talent. Paganini's concerts were more expensive than most, and he made deliberate use of his mystical reputation.[17] It seems he sought to foster his diabolic image in order to heighten audience interest. The marketing strategies of artists did not go unnoticed among contemporaries. Heinrich Heine analyses Liszt's success and his cult status with biting sarcasm. Many contemporaries had sought explanations in mystical powers but Heine's interpretation was more prosaic:

> It seems to me at times that all this sorcery may be explained by the fact that no one on earth knows so well how to organize his successes, or rather their *mise en scène*, as our Franz Liszt. In this art he is a genius, a Philadelphia, a Bosco, a Houdin, yes, a Meyerbeer! The most distinguished persons serve him gratis as his colleagues, and his hired enthusiasts are models of training. Popping champagne corks, and a reputation for prodigal generosity, trumpeted forth by the most reliable newspapers, lure recruits to him in every city.[18]

Liszt's genius was in his ability to stage his art, to make it into a spectacle in the manner of the famous illusionist Bosco and the opera composer Giacomo Meyerbeer. Heine certainly understood Liszt's virtuoso pianism but judged his fame to be as evanescent as was that of his rivals whose names soon disappeared from the annals of history. According to Heine's ironic prediction Liszt would in no time be reduced from the 'lion' to the 'rabbit', left to reminisce on his bygone glory:

> After all, their day of vain celebrity is a very short one, and the hour soon strikes when the titan of tonal art may, perhaps, crumple into a town musician of very dwarfish stature, who, in the coffee-house which he frequents, tells the regular guests, on his word of honour,

how bouquets of the most beautiful camelias were formerly flung at his feet, and how, once, two Hungarian countesses, in order to secure possession of his handkerchief, had cast themselves on the ground and fought until the blood ran. The day-long reputation of a virtuoso evaporates and dies away, empty, without a trace, like a camel's wind in the desert.[19]

The hysteria caused by stardom may have been transitory, yet there is a great deal that is new in the experience of contemporaries – not just the hysteria but also its critique. At the beginning of the nineteenth century newspapers became an influential disseminator of portrayals of public figures, faithfully spreading, as Heine notes, all possible details of their undertakings – news, announcements, advertisements, rumours, controversy. Music – like other art forms – gained momentum from the increasing power of the press. The institution of critique became established as the main arbiter of taste, and concerts and art exhibitions, as well as the latest literary works, became objects of public debate.

At the same time, musical societies established concert activities in larger cities on a regular basis. The hazy line between industrial culture and art is demonstrated by the conversion of the cloth traders' Gewandhaus (Clothiers' Hall) in Leipzig into a concert hall in 1781: instead of clothes, entrance fees now became the main product. Initially the hall at the Gewandhaus accommodated an audience of 500, and after the renovation and extension work in 1842 up to 1,000 music lovers. The Gewandhaus rose to international acclaim due to the concerts conducted by Felix Mendelssohn Bartholdy from the early 1830s onward. The concerts in Leipzig are remembered primarily for resurrecting Johann Sebastian Bach after a long period of oblivion.[20] Large concert halls also impacted on the music and its interpretation, as these open spaces required larger ensembles. During the century ever larger concert halls were constructed in the European metropolises; the Royal Albert Hall, completed in London between 1869 and 1871, can be seen as the culmination of this process, with seating capacity for 11,000 listeners. The megalomania went so far that it became impossible for a single conductor, raised onto a podium, to keep control over the players. Hector Berlioz's *Te Deum*

(1848–9) required a massive 900 performers and an additional 600 child singers. The orchestra included 100 strings, as well as fifty woodwind and fifty percussion instruments. Three choirs were also needed. It was impossible to direct such a huge machinery in a systematic manner without recourse to sub-conductors who led the performers according to instructions from the chief conductor, Berlioz himself. It is no wonder that Berlioz's method of conducting was termed militaristic.[21] One is inevitably reminded of the way in which work was generally organized in the nineteenth century. The industrial society had improved the rationalization and division of labour.

In the literary sphere the novel represented the new commercial and industrial age. Reading had become a popular pastime and the newspapers constantly needed new and imaginative tales for their audience. One of the most popular authors of the early nineteenth century was Alexandre Dumas senior (1802–70). He began his career as a playwright but turned to writing novels in the 1830s, particularly as the press craved for serial fiction to fill their columns. Dumas rewrote his play *Le Capitaine Paul* in prose form and practically became an industrial producer of novels: he gathered around him a production studio where a number of writers worked, exactly as musicians in an orchestra led by their conductor. In the ensuing decades one bestseller after another appeared – of these particularly *The Three Musketeers* (1844) and *The Count of Monte Cristo* (1845–6) have remained enduring favourites of adventure literature. While readers devoured these lively stories filled with unforeseen developments, the critics were dismayed. *The Count of Monte Cristo* – which was a *roman-feuilleton*, chopped into numerous small episodes – received a crushing review when it came out: it was considered both historically and psychologically inaccurate and the revenge exacted by the protagonist Edmond Dantès was interpreted as a threat to the social order.[22] At the same time, exaggerated imagination and passion for reading were deemed dangerous; unreserved surrender to the temptations of literature contained both moral and political risks.

The increasingly affluent middle class consumed literature and the changing literary scene provided opportunities for a renegotiation of the boundaries of publicity. Writing generated a new profession; besides authors, translators were also needed to promptly produce works for the reading hungry markets. In this situation also women were able to enter the literary scene and negotiate a new role for themselves. In Finland, the first novel was written by Fredrika Wilhelmina Carstens, whose *Murgrönan (Ivy)* appeared anonymously in 1840. There was, however, no doubt about the identity of the author and, being a woman, Carstens was clearly subjected to exceptionally harsh criticism. This novel, inspired by Jane Austen, was the only one she wrote. In Sweden, the author Fredrika Bremer (1801–65) also published her first works anonymously. When the books met with success with both readers and critics, however, Bremer came out and was even able to work independently, which was quite exceptional at the time. Bremer made long journeys on her own, going as far as the United States, and published her travelogue entitled *The Homes of the New World*.[23]

Although the enchantment and imaginativeness of art was criticized in the nineteenth century, art also had strong ties to social issues of the day. The time of the Napoleonic Wars had already produced visual contemporary commentary – a desire to deal with painful issues through the artistic medium. Francisco Goya (1746–1828) depicted the crucial moment of the Spanish war of liberation in his painting *The Third of May 1808: The Execution of the Defenders of Madrid*. The work was completed in 1814, after the defeat of Napoleon's army. Napoleon had hoped to establish his brother Joseph on the Spanish throne but the French offensive provoked spontaneous resistance, which was ruthlessly crushed, leading to the merciless execution of over 5,000 civilians. In Goya's painting, the French troops, depicted as an anonymous, implacable war machinery, shoot the civilians who participated in the popular uprising in Madrid. Goya also portrayed the horrors of war in a series of eighty aquatint prints, *Los desastres de la guerra (The Disasters of War)*, which were not, however, published until after his death.[24]

Goya had been a witness to political upheavals, but the art of the nineteenth century also anxiously sought refuge from an environment of cruelty. The Romantic artists were moved by the unbroken serenity of nature, a world beyond the storms and frenzy of everyday life. The Romantics were impressed with landscapes untouched or only transiently affected by humanity. In Germany, Caspar David Friedrich (1774–1840) described sublime natural scenes, people admiring the moonlit night, an autumn forest glowing with colours, abandoned buildings amid inspiring landscapes, or the sun setting into the Baltic Sea.[25]

Political unrest continued throughout the century and the French Revolutions of July 1830 and February 1848 inspired both writers and visual artists. In 1841, Heinrich Heine wrote in *Salon* magazine: 'Painting and sculpture, even architecture, took on a joyous uplift after the July Revolution, but the wings were only externally attached, and a deplorable fall succeeded the forced flight.'[26] The events of July inspired the painter Eugène Delacroix (1798–1863) to create one of his best-known pieces: *La Liberté guidant le peuple* (*Liberty Leading the People*). At the centre of the painting is a young woman of the people who has taken to the barricades. She is the personification of Liberty, the tricolour flying in her left hand, her right grasping an infantry musket. The soldiers visible behind Liberty are deliberately chosen to represent the bourgeoisie as well as lower classes, testifying to the broad social backing of the revolution. Although Delacroix's painting shows all the signs of Romanticism, strong colours and movement, the painting also alludes to tradition, to classical composition and the art of the Renaissance. Delacroix claimed he had joined the battle for his country with the painting. In October 1830 he wrote the following to his brother: 'I have undertaken a modern subject, a barricade, and if I have not fought for my country, at least I will paint for her.' The French government bought the painting with the intention of displaying it in the palace as a reminder to King Louis-Philippe that he had come to power by the will of the people. The painting proved to be too inflammatory, however, and was returned to the artist.[27]

The painting of the nineteenth century is generally remembered for a few key works, which have become familiar through numerous reproductions since the turn of the century. Much of the visual culture appreciated and consumed by the contemporaries has been lost and forgotten. Where portraits were regarded as an everyday consumable art form, the highest-ranking genre of visual arts since

the end of the seventeenth century had been that of history painting. After the Great Revolution in France, historical themes were
used to show connections with events of the recent past and to gen-
erate support for the regime. Artists like Delacroix were deter-
minedly opposed to this genre. Another expression of this
counter-culture was the practice of taking painting equipment out
of the studios, *en plein air*, and depicting phenomena and events in
natural light – a practice that gained popularity in the 1850s. In
France, the Barbizon school found inspiration in the work of the
English John Constable and, after the 1848 Revolution, moved into
the country to paint nature and the life of the peasants. One of the
movement's most famous works was Jean-François Millet's *The
Gleaners* from 1857.[28] Painting outdoors became important not only
to Realists like Millet but later also to the Impressionists. This movement derived its name from Claude Monet's work *Impression: Sunrise*
from 1873. The artist's aim was to capture an impression that was
more a play of light and colour than an outline of the proportions
of an object seen. The pursuit of subjective internal experience and
the deliberate testing of artistic boundaries became all-important.[29]

Interest in the visual arts increased during the nineteenth century
in much the same way as interest in literature and music. Music permeated the everyday in the form of parlour music and concerts, and
visual arts reached the gentry in particular in the collections of galleries and museums. There was also a renewed interest in the old
masters and art history. The collections of the Louvre were con-
verted into a public museum in 1793, immediately following the
Revolution. The collections were added to as Napoleon's victori-
ous troops hoarded more treasures for the museum. The founding
of the Louvre set an example for other European collections. The
Prado in Madrid was opened in 1819 but, due to insufficient space,
only a small portion of the works collected and received by the
Spanish kings during the course of history could be displayed. Over
the century national museums and national art collections became
the links by means of which a country's national cultural heritage
was connected to international developments. They became vehi-
cles for memory and remembrance.[30]

At the same time as museums made artistic experiences more
widely accessible, the singularity of experience was also stressed.

Historians of the nineteenth century, like the Swiss Jacob Burckhardt in his *The Civilization of the Renaissance in Italy* (1860), focused on the flourishing periods of past civilizations. The achievements of the ancient world and the Renaissance became part of the western artistic canon, sacred objects to which travellers should sojourn, particularly if their travels took them to Greece or Italy. Although such art treasures were absent as achievements of the lost world of the past, they were still accessible through cultural travel.

The nineteenth century produced travel writing by the metre, if not by the libraryful, and it was Italy, in particular, whose role as the birthplace of art gained prominence. Johann Wolfgang von Goethe's description of his journey to Italy was eagerly consumed by readers throughout the century. Another influential traveller was the French author Stendhal (1783–1842). He had travelled widely in Europe and even participated in Napoleon's Russian campaign. He left for Italy in 1817, describing in his work *Naples and Florence: A Journey from Milan to Reggio* the powerful emotions Florence inspired in him. The wonders of Florence overwhelmed Stendhal, even to the extent of causing physical reactions:

> My soul, affected by the very notion of being in Florence, and by the proximity of those great men whose tombs I had just beheld, was already in a state of trance. Absorbed in the contemplation of *sublime beauty*, I could perceive its very essence close at hand; I could, as it were, feel the stuff of it beneath my fingertips. I had attained to that supreme degree of sensibility where the *divine intimations* of art merge with the impassioned sensuality of emotion. As I emerged from the porch of *Santa Croce*, I was seized with a fierce palpitation of the heart (the same symptom which, in Berlin, is referred to as an *attack of nerves*); the well-spring of life was dried up within me, and I walked in constant fear of falling to the ground.[31]

The experiences described by Stendhal, the accelerated pulse and dizziness, have later also been associated with encounters with art treasures. Stendhal's syndrome, as these symptoms have later become known, was not diagnosed until 1979, however, and is most common among travellers to Florence, particularly among women travelling alone.[32] Although Stendhal's syndrome was

unknown as a medical term in the nineteenth century, encounters
with art did create a fierce emotional experience, a passion, perhaps
related to the manic desire to own books, described by Gustave
Flaubert in his short story *Bibliomanie* (1836). The nineteenth
century was a century of collecting and the search for sensations.[33]

Although nineteenth-century European culture was still in
many respects a religious one, the role of religion had gradually
diminished. Experiences of art and of the sublime in historical surroundings may still have generated a rapture akin to experiencing
the sacred. At least Stendhal described his experiences in Florence
by referring to religion: 'The tide of emotion which overwhelmed
me flowed so deep that it scarce was to be distinguished from religious awe.'[34] The American poet and author Bayard Taylor (1825–
78) journeyed to Italy in the 1840s and described in detail the
mysterious atmosphere of the *duomo* in Florence:

> I attended service in the Cathedral one dark, rainy morning, and was
> never before so deeply impressed with the majesty and grandeur of the
> mighty edifice. The thick, cloudy atmosphere darkened still more the
> light which came through the stained windows, and a solemn twilight
> reigned in the long aisles. The mighty dome sprang far aloft, as if it
> inclosed a part of heaven, for the light that straggled through the
> windows around its base, lay in broad bars on the blue, hazy air. I should
> not have been surprised at seeing a cloud float within it. The lofty burst
> of the organ boomed echoing away through dome and nave, with a
> chiming, metallic vibration, shaking the massive pillars which it would
> defy an earthquake to rend. All was wrapped in dusky obscurity, except
> where, in the side-chapels, crowns of tapers were burning around the
> images. One knows not which most to admire, the genius which could
> conceive, or the perseverance which could accomplish such a work.[35]

Not all travellers were as understanding or equally impressed,
however. Taylor's compatriot George Stillman Hillard (1808–79)
was openly disappointed with the coarse exterior of Florence's
Santa Croce:

> I went to the church of Santa Croce in the expectation of seeing some-
> thing externally imposing and beautiful. The Westminster Abbey of

Florence I supposed would have something noble and majestic in its aspect, not unworthy of the illustrious dead who have been committed to its charge; but what was my disappointment when I saw a mere mountain of brick, with as little pretension to beauty or proportion as the gable of a barn, – an ugly, unfinished facade, more suggestive of a cotton factory than a church. The interior is venerable and imposing, dimly lighted by long and narrow Gothic windows of stained glass, and shrouded in the gloom which seems appropriate to a church of which the chief interest is in its tombs and its monuments.[36]

The experience of art was intertwined with a broader experience of history, of the past as a sensation that could only be attained at centres such as Florence, in the vicinity of the tombs of Michelangelo, Dante and Galilei. Hillard's illusion was shattered by an unforeseen association with the contemporary and familiar industrial culture of his homeland: the sacred object that he had passionately awaited to encounter reminded him, bewilderingly, of a cotton mill. In the traveller's experience opposites became merged. Hence, at a time when European society was modernizing, it was also turning into a museum piece, petrifying into a theatre of memory.[37] It became charged with a longing for a past that would never return and that modern culture was casting aside.

4

On the Cultural History of Nationalism

During the nineteenth century, nationalism was one of the most powerful, and successful, political forces. Nationalism deeply influenced western thought and shaped the map of Europe. Although in many ways an heir of the French Revolution, it became significant in its own right. It was not only an ideology, with a coherent way of thinking, but was also a means of seeing the individual in relation to society and provided a way of re-creating that relationship and constructing patriotic sentiments, with a sense of belonging and community. Nationalism is often viewed in terms of politics, but it was in many ways a cultural historical phenomenon, loaded with meanings, signs and symbols. It has left its imprint on the arts, popular culture, historical understanding, education – and emotions.

Nationalism is generally perceived as a product of the turn of the nineteenth century. Before then, the inhabitants of states, cities and towns had of course felt a love or even patriotism for their native land but the concept of a nation, united by a common language, customs, characteristics and geography, did not become significant in European culture until the beginning of the nineteenth century. After the Great Revolution in France, the idea of a citizens' community received a powerful impetus: the community itself could be a force for political change. If power was not invested in the crown or the aristocracy but in the people, then what exactly was meant by the people and who were included?[1] The concept of citizenship (*citoyen*) became a core issue in the French Revolution. It was used in determining the political rights available to each member of the community. Although citizenship, in principle, affected all, it should be remembered that in practice women were not accepted as equals in decision-making. Even though such activists as Olympe de Gouges, Mary Wollstonecraft and Théodore de Hippel had argued already at the end of the eighteenth century that all sexes were equal, and de Gouges even published her *Déclaration des droits de la femme et de la citoyenne* in 1791, women were excluded from political power for the whole of the nineteenth century.[2] On the level of rhetoric, the 'nation as a whole' was spoken of, yet, in practice, national cultures were determined by men. In addition, the 'people' of nationalism were more an ideal than a real image, with the cultural elite playing a central role in its construction.

Research has found it difficult to define the multifaceted concept of 'nationalism'. One terminological approach is to refer to the original Latin meaning of the term. In antiquity, a goddess named Natio was known, who protected women during childbirth. The meaning of birth or origin has been attached to the derivatives of the word at later times too. If people belong to the same nation, they are assumed to have a common origin. In early modern times, the word 'natio' was used in various ways to signify not only the place of birth but also other communities, the guild-system of foreign merchants, as well as university fraternities. The concept 'nation' acquired, however, its political significance in the nineteenth century.[3] According to Ernest Gellner, there was in fact a close linkage between nationalism and the rise of the modern industrial society. Industrial growth required cultural standardization: nations and citizens were much needed components in the modern, fluid world where economic and cultural exchange played a crucial role.[4]

Although the transformation of national belonging into the ideology of nationalism has been approached in various ways, the most practical can be found in the historian Eric J. Hobsbawm's characterization: a nation is 'any sufficiently large body of people

whose members regard themselves as members of a "nation"'.[5]
Ultimately the most important question is how a given community perceives and regards itself. On this view, reality and imagination become intertwined to form an inseparable whole. The
question of national imagination has been discussed influentially by
Benedict Anderson in his book *Imagined Communities* in which he
defines the modern nation as an imaginary community.[6] That is, a
community that is not necessarily real. In fact, Anderson says that
all communities larger than villages inevitably base themselves on
imagination, on an assumption of unity. Those who belong to a
nation can never know the other members personally. They are
tied together as a nation by symbolic, and sometimes possibly even
invented, factors. Many national traditions that are perceived to
have their roots in history, such as the national standard languages,
are in fact relatively recent inventions. Even though nations have
been built from above, they cannot be analysed only from the perspective of elites. Especially in the study of national identity it is
essential to pay attention to popular sentiments and imagination:
what kind of presuppositions, hopes, needs and desires were
attached to nationality.[7]

Although imagination and the invention of tradition have always
played an important role in national thought and activities, a central
rhetorical strategy has been to present nationalist endeavours as
natural and inevitable. It has been of crucial political significance
to emphasize the compatibility of the state and its people. The
German theorist Johann Gottfried Herder had already written of
'the natural state' when speaking of a nation-state that has, in effect,
formed around its population. According to this way of thinking,
communities followed a natural evolution, with harmony between
the people, nation and state at its end.[8]

Eric J. Hobsbawm has divided the history of nationalist thinking into two periods, those of Mazzinian nationalism and political
state nationalism. The nationalism named after the Italian Giuseppe
Mazzini (1805–72) is, according to Hobsbawm, characterized by
a so-called 'threshold principle' that requires a nation to be
sufficiently large to form a state. At the same time, a nation must
have a historical link with a state, either with one that exists or one
with a long history. The nation must also have a social class that is

devoted to the preservation of culture and upholds an administrative language as well as a national literature. A third important criterion was a tested ability for conquest, in other words, a military and political maturity. The nationalism conceptualized by Mazzini was, in Hobsbawm's view, the primary form of nationalist ideology until the 1880s and its best examples were German and Italian nationalism. In the 1880s, a shift occurred towards a new kind of state-centred nationalism, which no longer endorsed the threshold principle. Even a small community could demand the establishment of a nation-state on any territory on the basis of the principle of national autonomy. At the same time ethnic and linguistic criteria became dominant in defining a nation. Where Mazzinian nationalism had emphasized the role of a cultural elite, the masses were now given a political significance. Belonging to a nation became almost a popular religion, and its propagation was facilitated by the educational system.[9]

Although the new state-centred nationalism strongly emphasized the role of the people and their rights in decision-making, the people as a concept was central to all nationalistic discourse. Herder had already emphasized that the soul of a people was to be found in its folk songs and popular stories. Folklore was seen to reflect the anonymous, collective spirit of a people, which the Germans called its *Volksgeist*.[10] Thus the innermost essence of a nation could be revealed by becoming versed with the heritage collected from its people. From our contemporary perspective it is easy to question the existence of any such 'authentic populace'. Aren't the people as a whole always an imaginary construct? Does folklore not tell us as much about the world of its collector as that of its subjects? It was typical in Mazzinian nationalism that the cultural elite, the cultured bourgeoisie, took a keen interest in popular culture. Their interest effected a filtering process, where disadvantageous ingredients were happily forgotten, whereas noble and dignified elements were emphasized. There has always been an abundance of vulgar and indecent accounts, poems and expressions in folk tradition, yet these had no place in nationalist idealizations. In his novel *From the Life of a Good-for-Nothing* (*Aus dem Leben eines Taugenichts*, 1826), Joseph von Eichendorff has strikingly portrayed the way the gentility idealized the people. The main character in the novel meets an upper-class party, who ask the on-comer for a folksong. Eichendorff writes:

> While I was gazing at her, it suddenly occurred to the other lady, the plump happy one, that I should sing something during the trip. A very elegant young gentleman with spectacles on his nose, who was sitting by her, turned towards her quickly, kissed her hand gently and said, 'What a clever idea! A folk-song, sung by the people themselves in the open fields and woods, is like an Alpine rose which is actually growing on the Alps. It is the soul of our nation, while *Magic Horns* are mere collections of dried plants.' But I said I had nothing to sing which was worthy of such a noble company.[11]

Collectors of folklore found role models in the German authors and researchers, Johann Gottfried Herder, the brothers Grimm or Achim von Arnim and Clemens Brentano who had published their famous collection of folksongs *Des Knaben Wunderhorn* (*The Boy's Magic Horn*) in 1805–8. In Finland, their example was followed by Elias Lönnrot who collected the folk poems of the *Kanteletar* as well as the epic *Kalevala*. Later research on the sources has shown that Lönnrot censored folk poems that he felt were immoral, selected from the versions he had collected those that conformed to his artistic vision and, when necessary, even recomposed verses in order to create an epical whole. It was not a case of Lönnrot discovering the epos ready-made, and nor had the *Kalevala* ever existed in the form given to it by Lönnrot. It was clearly more a product of Lönnrot's artistic abilities than those of the 'Finnish people'. Lönnrot's relation to the *Kalevala* is not only a reflection of Finnish culture, however, since similar situations are to be found throughout nineteenth-century Europe. The cultural bourgeoisie did not simply construct a picture of the people but also of its past and its mythology. Artists straightforwardly imitated the style of folk poems and folk tunes, sometimes even intentionally creating fakes of which *The Poems of Ossian*, penned by James MacPherson in the 1760s, are an excellent example. MacPherson insisted on having collected the Celtic poem from the traditions he had found in the Scottish highlands, whereas, in reality, he had composed the work himself, inspired by the aesthetic of early Romanticism.[12]

Enthusiasm for folklore is only one, and in itself quite limited, perspective on the cultural historical impact of nationalism. The nationalist ideology was apparent in cultural production in ways other than imitation. Interest in history was especially strong during the nineteenth century. In addition to historical research, the past permeated paintings and novels as well as plays and operas. In early German nineteenth-century nationalism, historical settings were unavoidable since the occupation by the Napoleonic armies denied the opportunity for political critique except when historically disguised. Friedrich Schiller, for example, deals allegorically with the French occupation in his plays *Jungfrau von Orleans* (1801) and *Wilhelm Tell* (1804). The same is true of Heinrich von Kleist's play *Hermannsschlacht* (1808). The German drama of the early nineteenth century has occasionally been described as a social laboratory in which the possibilities for political resistance could be tested and practised.[13]

In literary novels, imagined national histories were also plentiful and popular. Until the latter half of the nineteenth century the Scottish author Sir Walter Scott (1771–1832) served as a role model for many as his work, besides its tremendous impact on Scottish historical consciousness, also profoundly influenced the whole of European literature. In the Nordic countries one of the heirs of the Scottian novel is Zachris Topelius's expansive series of novels *Tales of a Field Surgeon* (*Fältskärns berättelser*), which initially appeared as a serial story in the Swedish-language newspaper *Helsingfors Tidningar* between 1853 and 1866.[14] The world presented by the story has, especially in Sweden and Finland, left an indelible mark on both literature and historical consciousness; its effects were discernible all the way up to the Second World War. The novel begins in the midst of the Thirty Years War in the seventeenth century and continues until the murder of the Swedish King Gustavus III at the end of the eighteenth century. Topelius tells the story of Sweden's role as a great power alongside a Finnish family narrative. In the history of Finnish nationalism, Topelius represented a strongly Swedish-sympathizing tendency. Finland had come under Russian rule in 1809, but in his art Topelius wanted to emphasize the historical ties between Sweden and Finland. Thus Topelius took part in constructing a Finnish history that was an inseparable part of the undertakings of western Europe.

The conception of history applied in Zachris Topelius's novel could in many ways be taken as representative of nineteenth-century European thought. At the centre of the story is a ring that brings power, quite like that of Wagner's *The Ring of the Nibelung*. The theme of the ring is ultimately entwined with Topelius's conception of providence. Forged by a Finnish witch, the magic object finds its way to the royal finger to finally dictate national destinies. Gustavus II Adolphus loses the bronze ring shortly before his death, as does Charles XII just before his luck turns. The adventures of the ring among Finnish peasants and Swedish royalty serve to emphasize Topelius's conception of the shared historical destiny of Finland and Sweden. In this sense, Topelius's novel belongs in the realm of Mazzinian nationalism. The aim is one of unification, a demonstration that Finland is not part of Russian culture. Another significant feature in Topelius's vision is his faith in the individual, in a strong leader who is obeyed by his subjects. In addition to providing a field for the unfolding of the national spirit, history is also a stage for great men. According to Topelius, Charles XII, the warrior king of Sweden, was 'like a mountain amidst the dwarves of his time, on his shoulders alone lay this epoch that fell with him and will never rise from its grave'.[15]

Faith in great men was a typical feature of nationalist culture. These included not only the great figures involved in historical events but also the artists themselves. Especially German Romanticism emphasized that the spirit of a people could be channelled in the works of individual artists as well as in tradition. The people could speak through its genius. According to this way of thinking an individual could interpret the sentiments of an entire nation, Zachris Topelius those of the Finns, Richard Wagner of the Germans, Giuseppe Verdi of the Italians, or Mihail Glinka of the Russians. The idea was taken furthest by Richard Wagner (1813–83) who perceived his views on art to be essentially German: musical drama (Wagner's favoured form of composition) was the German art form par excellence. In many of his writings he claimed that only he had understood how German culture could rise from its state of degradation and how art could become a unifying force for the nation. The fusion of Wagner's interpretation of the national spirit and the idea of the genius is well exemplified by a quote from his diary, written by the composer in 1865. In this excerpt he refers to the nationalist aspirations of the *Burschenschafts*, sports organizations founded by German students:

> Then came the *Burschenschaft*. The League of Virtue was founded. All so fantastic that no human being could grasp it. But I have grasped it. Now it is *me* whom no one grasps. I am the most German being. I am the German spirit. Question the incomparable magic of *my* works – compare them with the rest and you can for the time being say no differently than that – it is *German*! But what is this *German*? It must be something wonderful, mustn't it, for it is humanly finer than all else? – Oh heavens! It should have a soil, *this German*! I should be able to find my people! What a glorious people it ought to become. But to this people only could I belong.[16]

Germanity appears in this quotation as unique and original, as something beyond compare. The fragment ends on the claim that this Germanity 'should have a soil'. Mazzinian nationalism, which the excerpt can be linked to, was of a unifying nature. It was also Wagner's goal that Germany, politically fragmented as it was, could be unified into a nation-state, something that in fact took place in 1871, six years after the above excerpt from his journal was written. Despite these affinities, the egocentricity of Wagner's words is striking. Although he writes of belonging and being German, the whole text centres on the 'I'. In writing: 'I am the most German being. I am the German spirit,' Wagner sees himself as the interpreter of the national spirit.[17]

Nationalist rhetoric was forcefully present in the arts culture of the nineteenth century. Artists either proclaimed themselves to be the mouthpieces of their nation or they were transformed into symbolic figures, interpreters of the nation. Richard Wagner was an exceptional icon among these artists. He was, without doubt, one of the most interesting Europeans of the nineteenth century and his works and thoughts still awaken conflicting feelings, perhaps because the conflicts within Europeans seem to draw together in his person. Wagner was an ardent nationalist yet also defended universalism. He expounded on the importance of 'common humanity' but tended towards extreme racism. He participated in the democratic revolution in the spring of 1849 in the wake of Europe's 'year of revolutions' but he also later became a conservative, nearly a predecessor to the Nazis.

Wagner's most notable artistic contributions were his operas, works like the *Flying Dutchman, Tannhäuser, Lohengrin, Tristan and Isolde, The Mastersingers of Nuremberg, The Ring of the Nibelung* and *Parsifal.* For a long time, Wagner inspired resistance in his contemporaries, and musical circles in the 1840s were divided into Wagnerians and anti-Wagnerians, supporters and opponents. At stake was not only a musical or artistic but also a political issue. Wagner himself was unwilling to draw a line between these spheres: 'No one now can poetise, without politising.'[18] In a sense, Wagner articulated a thought that often remained unsaid in nationalist art. If an artist shaped the views of the nation and national objectives, it was necessarily a case of political action: the artist became a politician. Wagner himself thirsted for the status of a national icon. In the 1860s he thought that Germany could be unified under the rule of Bavaria. This was not to be, however. Before long, Wagner realized that the motive power behind change was not to be the young king of Bavaria, Ludwig II, but the iron chancellor of Prussia, Otto von Bismarck. When Wagner realized this in the summer of 1866, he began to look for contacts in Berlin. On the eve of the German unification, Wagner finally achieved the success he had longed for on the opera stage with his *Mastersingers of Nuremberg* (*Die Meistersinger von Nürnberg*). The piece can well be seen as the musical equivalent of Wagner's collection of articles in *Deutsche Kunst und Deutsche Politik* which he wrote during the autumn of 1867 and which appeared as a book the following spring. Both dealt passionately with the connection between art and politics. Wagner completed the score for the *Mastersingers* in October 1867, at the same time as he was writing his series of articles for the *Süddeutsche Presse* newspaper. The opera premiered in the summer of the following year, at the time when *Deutsche Kunst und Deutsche Politik* became available as a book.[19]

The opera is set in sixteenth-century Nuremberg where master singer festivals are being celebrated. At the beginning of the opera, goldsmith Veit Pogner's daughter Eva falls in love with the young knight Walther von Stolzing, who is only visiting Nuremberg. Pogner has, however, decided that Eva is to be the prize in the mid-summer song competition. The suggestion by the cobbler Hans Sachs that the winner be selected by general acclaim is rejected. The decision is left in the hands of the judges. One of the judges is the scribe Sixtus Beckmesser, who also dreams of Eva. During the night Walther has a beautiful dream and creates a poem for a new master song. Before this, Walther has already failed the audition and lost his chances of participating in the competition. Hans Sachs gives the verses that Walther has composed to Beckmesser, offering him 'the keys to victory'. Beckmesser naturally fails in the competition since the song is not his own: his style is wrong. Sachs suggests that Walther be allowed to present the song even though he failed the trial round. Walther sings a wonderful aria ('Morgenlicht leuchtend in rosigem Schein . . .') and naturally wins. He refuses to accept the title of master singer but wins his heart's beloved, Eva. The opera ends on a finale where Hans Sachs sings the praises of the German masters:

> Beware! Evil tricks threaten us;
> if the German people and kingdom should one day decay,
> under a false, foreign rule
> soon no prince will understand his people any more;
> and foreign mists with foreign vanities
> they will plant in our German land;
> what is German and true no one would know any more,
> if it did not live in the honour of the German Masters.
> Therefore I say to you;
> honour your German Masters,
> then you will conjure up good spirits!
> And if you favour their endeavours,
> even should the
> Holy Roman Empire dissolve in mist,
> for us there would yet remain
> holy German Art![20]

It seems that Wagner wished to anchor himself in the tradition of the 'German masters' with this opera.[21] In much the same way that the master singers of the sixteenth century were forced to struggle against foreign cultural influence, Wagner had to do battle for the sake of German art. Wagner probably identified intensely with the character of Hans Sachs. This is indicated, for example, by the fact that he often signed his letters with the name Hans Sachs, especially if writing on matters connected to the *Mastersingers*.[22]

In the opera, Hans Sachs suggests that the people, not the judges, be allowed to decide who is the best master singer. This is in accord with the opinion that Wagner had of critics. From the point of view of the art, the decisive question was how it served the community not the renown it received from the critics. Indeed, Beckmesser was clearly a caricature of the kind of biased and narrow-minded critic who tried to imitate the old, traditional style but was doomed to make a fool of himself. The model for Beckmesser was Eduard Hanslick, the music critic of the Viennese newspaper *Neue Freie Presse*.

The most important thing about the *Mastersingers of Nuremberg* was its zealous patriotism which greatly appealed to the German audience. After its Munich premiere, the *Mastersingers* spread quickly around Germany, playing in many opera houses on the very eve of the Franco–Prussian war in 1870. The 'false, foreign rule' (*falsche welsche Majestät*) shown by Hans Sachs appears to have been a direct reference to the corrupting influence of French civilization that had to be forcefully countered. In this way Wagner's opera received immediate contemporary significance.

When Germany was unified in January 1871, Wagner was ready to step forth as the nation's leading artistic icon. He even composed a piece entitled the *Kaisermarsch* that he hoped would become the national anthem of the new Germany. However, the unified Germany never rose to the challenge set by Wagner, and his art failed to receive official national recognition. In the end, Wagner was forced to found the Bayreuth music festival with money that he raised and received in donations. Wagner had been so successful in promoting himself as the national icon that many of his contemporaries thought of him as the Imperial composer. When Karl Marx passed through Bayreuth on his way to Leipzig in 1876 he wrote to Friedrich Engels that the town was celebrating the 'carnival of the state musician'.[23]

The Italian opera composer Giuseppe Verdi (1813–1901) could well be compared to Richard Wagner as a national symbol, although he never provoked equally conflicting emotions in his contemporaries as did his German colleague. As a composer, Verdi was quite distinct from Wagner even though the two shared an interest in nationalist themes. Like Wagner, Verdi also admitted the connection between art and politics. In fact, he often sought themes for his operas that he felt to have political significance. Censorship was strict, however, hampering the treatment of delicate themes.

During the restoration following the Napoleonic Wars, the rulers of the Italian principalities used all possible means to prevent the spread of new ideas. The Austrians, who controlled Venice and Lombardy, were particularly wary of themes that related to opposition of rulers, conspiracies or assassinations – themes that were, in fact, very dear to Italian opera. In Naples, censors had a very different emphasis, paying more attention to religious and moral questions. Censorship was harshest in Rome, where authors were required to submit librettos to censors in forty-one copies. Because of such strict control, librettists avoided contemporary themes and situated their stories in the distant past. It was a matter of interaction between authors and their audiences. Opera-goers were accustomed to interpreting periphrases and understood the political content relating to the unification of Italy despite the censorship. In part, this was due to the nature of the inspection of librettos. Expressions used in a text did not, as such, reveal the forcefulness with which they would be presented in the performance. There is a scene in Verdi's *Attila* (1846) where the Roman general Ezio is conducting negotiations with the leader of the Huns, Attila. They belt out a duet, in which Ezio suggests for Attila to 'take the world, but leave me Italy!' The censors did not recognize the fact that in Attila's time there was no Italy but only the Roman Empire. For emphasis, the last words of the duet are repeated so many times that the audience gets to hear 'Italy' a total of fourteen times. The audience was able to interpret the Huns as an allegory of the Austrians. Legend has it that on the opening night the audience burst out shouting 'Leave us Italy!' after the duet and the composer was carried in triumphal procession to his hotel.[24]

Verdi's most obvious political opera was the *Battle of Legnano* (*La battaglia di Legnano*) which premiered in Rome in 1849. At the time the Pope was in exile and Rome was experiencing a short-lived republic. The opera told the story of how, in the twelfth century, Italians defeated Fredrik Barbarossa in the battle of Legnano. The audience was especially moved by a scene in which the hero Arrigo jumps from a tower shouting 'Viva Italia!' After the fall of the Republic of Rome, the opera was not performed again until the unification of Italy when the piece was presented as one of the symbolic works of the Risorgimento.[25]

While the significance of symbolic figures like Verdi and Wagner was manifold, they participated, above all, in the construction of images and conceptions of the nation and of nationhood. In a nationalist culture, imagination was both synchronic and diachronic. Synchronic thinking emphasized situating the nation in relation to surrounding cultures and other nations. Diachronic thinking, on the other hand, emphasized the importance of historical continuity: the nation had 'always' been. The days of its magnificence could be long past, but glory could be returned if the nation realized its own station and significance. The diachronous approach ensured the popularity of historically focused art, which indeed continued in Europe throughout the nineteenth century. The subjects of operas were systematically sought for in the past. Wagner and Verdi are excellent examples of this. This past could well be mythical, as in Wagner's *The Ring of the Nibelung*, or historical, as in Verdi's *A Masked Ball*.

It was particularly in the sphere of Mazzinian nationalism that imagining the past was emphasized. This was also a matter of constructing symbolic capital for the nation. Suitable building blocks were found in customs and rituals, heraldry and flags as well as landscapes and images that were considered national. The politics of symbols was also important in the later forms of nationalism, yet at the end of the nineteenth century participation and activating the populace were foregrounded. This was linked to a transformation in the nature of nationalism at the end of the century. When participation became a significant aspect of defining citizenship, some means of providing a connection between citizens and the state were also needed. In this situation the nationalist ideology sought strength in folk celebrations, the power of masses and a sense of belonging. The role of sports in increasing levels of participation grew significantly even though physical training and gymnastics had also previously had an important place (the German *Burschenschafts* since the 1840s, for example). In England, football became an important working-class sport at the turn of the century, finding its home in the football clubs that had quickly appeared around the country. Sports competitions – and especially international matches – became forums for national deeds of heroism as well as for symbolic battles between nations. Although sports became a major generator of team spirit, it also paradoxically emphasized difference: sports divided people according to gender as well as class. In the beginning, working-class women had no share, whereas upper-class women could partake in activities like tennis and cycling.

Another paradox lies in the fact that sports also became a symbol of international peace and cooperation. The first modern Olympics were held in Athens in 1896, yet international disagreements were present from the very beginning. The Germans felt the attitude of the first chairman of the Olympic committee, Pierre de Coubertin, to be insulting: he had – or so the story goes – urged French competitors to seek revenge through sport for the wounds received in the Franco–Prussian war some twenty years earlier. A second point that undermined the atmosphere of peace was the relation of the first host country, Greece, to its eastern neighbour: Turkey refused to send a team to Athens.[26] This may have reflected a more general problem connected with nationalism. A strong national we-spirit had been constructed since the end of the nineteenth century but a by-product of the nationalist ideology – which had almost become a national religion – was a growing inability to understand the thoughts and feelings of others. Intolerance increased in Europe during the last decades of the nineteenth century while, at the same time, racial doctrines confirmed ideas of ethnic solidarity. Simultaneously, European culture was becoming strongly family-oriented. The safe world of the home and of biological kinship surfaced as central starting points for social values.

5

A Century of Family and Home: Daily Routines and Country Excursions

O Christmas Tree! O Christmas Tree!
Thy candles shine so brightly!
O Christmas Tree! O Christmas Tree!
Thy candles shine so brightly!
From base to summit, gay and bright,
There's only splendour for the sight.
O Christmas Tree! O Christmas Tree!
Thy candles shine so brightly!

These verses are from the famous Christmas carol that became popular in Germany under the title 'O Tannenbaum'. The song was based on a German folk tune and penned by the Leipzig organist Ernst Anschütz in 1824.[1] It evokes an image of a nineteenth-century family: children gathered around the Christmas tree were part of the bourgeois family ideal. At Christmas, the poor and the wealthy all lived together in accord, peace was in the land and harmony prevailed. And at the centre of this picture was, before all, the nuclear family, the father, the mother and the children, whose solidarity was emphasized in the Christmas celebrations with their family meals and ceremonies. Although the Christ Child was also part of the Christmas tradition, and many of the carols celebrated 'the newborn King', Christmas actually changed from a Christian, religious holiday to a celebration of children and family.[2] In practice, European Christmas traditions found their current form during the nineteenth century. Whereas Goethe was thunderstruck to see a Christmas tree at the home of a friend in Leipzig in 1765, already by the first half of the nineteenth century this Scandinavian custom had spread through Germany to France and England. By the end of the century the custom was so well established that the French sent decorated fir trees to residents of their African colonies.[3]

The establishment of Christmas celebrations is closely linked with changes in the meaning of the family during the nineteenth century. The social break brought on by industrial culture formed the backdrop. Private life had also changed. While the central social unit of agrarian communities was kinfolk, the family became more important to urban culture. The nineteenth century has indeed been called the century of the family:[4] it marked the birth of the nuclear family in its twentieth-century sense. On the other hand, the lifestyles of families in industrial society varied greatly according to their social group. The lifestyle of working-class families differed significantly from that of the bourgeoisie.[5]

The home became a private haven, a counterpoint to both public life and the continually changing sensory environment of industrial society. During the end of the eighteenth century and the beginning of the nineteenth, western countries experienced a structural change in public life. The press had become a central player in influencing public opinion, as well as an arena for political debate and the formation of public opinion. In this world of politicized publicity the home was a refuge where the private self could hide when the occasion warranted. This should not, however, be taken too literally. In the nineteenth century, as in the centuries before and after, the living rooms, sitting rooms and salons of private homes were also public rather than completely private spaces. Homes had a public and social function.[6] It is interesting, however, that the significance of homes seems to have been emphasized in the context of the political and industrial culture of the nineteenth century. Especially in the early part of the century, industrial society developed almost completely without social control. Although cities became polluted and noise levels rose, environmental thinking was only just beginning to emerge. In his novel *Oliver Twist*, published in 1838, Charles Dickens describes London as an unpleasantly sensory experience:

> A dirtier or more wretched place he [Oliver] had never seen. The street was very narrow and muddy, and the air was impregnated with filthy odours. There were a good many small shops; but the only stock in trade appeared to be heaps of children, who, even at that time of night, were crawling in and out at the doors, or screaming from the inside. The sole places that seemed to prosper amid the general blight of the place, were the public-houses; and in them, the lowest orders of Irish were wrangling with might and main. Covered ways and yards, which here and there diverged from the main street, disclosed little knots of houses, where drunken men and women were positively wallowing in filth; and from several of the door-ways, great ill-looking fellows were cautiously emerging, bound, to all appearance, on no very well-disposed or harmless errands.[7]

Although the novel romanticizes the misery of London's poorer districts, it also summarizes feelings brought on by the environmental effects that followed the Industrial Revolution. Especially the outskirts and suburbia of urban centres changed. Guy de Maupassant (1850–93) depicts the harsh imprint of industrialization in his 1881 short story 'A Day in the Country':

> The sun began to burn their faces; the dust got into their eyes all the time, and on both sides of the road the land spread out, interminably bare, dirty, and foul-smelling. It looked as though it had been ravaged by leprosy which had even eaten into the houses, for the skeletons of deserted tumbledown buildings, even a number of small villas left unfinished because the builders had not been paid, held out four walls but no roofs. Here and there, tall factory chimneys sprouted from the sterile ground, the only things that grew in these mouldering fields where the spring breezes wafted a scent of oil and slag-heaps mixed with another, even less pleasant odour.[8]

The smell of oil and slag is a by-product of material success in Maupassant's short story. The story itself follows a bourgeois

Parisian family on their outing to the clean countryside, to the peace and quiet of nature, away from the noise of the city and the 'tall factory chimneys'.

The French historian Alain Corbin has called the nineteenth century 'the century of linen' as a counterweight to its industrial effects.[9] At the same time as the sensory environment changed for the worse, linen made its way to private homes, and, by the end of the century, even to those of the working class. Underwear and domestic linens offered sensory pleasure and softness in the age of hard technology. The world of the home was protected against the misery outside by pampering the skin, by caring for the body that had become a central production factor in the altered working life. The home was provided with a sensory aura in other ways also. The 'scent of slag' and decay from the streets was replaced inside the home with mild perfumes, herbs and flowers, freshly baked pastries, the indefinable yet unparalleled fragrance of the home treated the olfactory nerves.

Amid the growing wretchedness of the physical environment, homes became a means for controlling the milieu. In their own house or residence a family was allowed – at least in principle – to create the kind of living environment they wanted. Especially the bourgeoisie spent both money and effort on their surroundings; the working classes had far less possibility for decorating. Ways of urban living formed a new kind of divide: the working classes lived in modest conditions whereas the lives of the bourgeoisie became sumptuously home-oriented.[10]

The dwellings of the nobility provided remote examples for middle-class homes. These homes were generally lavishly decorated, wallpapers were ornamental and the walls were filled with pictures, both paintings and photographs. The bourgeoisie became a significant consumer of art and there was a market for both copies of well-known pieces as well as for inexpensive reproductions. Copies of masterpieces lent the bourgeois home a cultural atmosphere while at the same time strengthening the impression of the importance of kitsch in middle-class sensibility. The concept of kitsch has its origins in the turn-of-the-century expression *etwas verkitschen* which meant selling products at cut-rate prices.[11] After the First World War, the term was used to refer to the bad or the tasteless in art. The targets of this pejorative expression were often the copies that had become popular during the nineteenth century and which the bourgeoisie used in giving a cultured image of itself. Occasionally, the concept of kitsch was also used to refer – in addition to replicas – to everyday ornamental objects such as the lampshades or coatracks that formed an essential part of the decoration of the Victorian home.[12]

Life within the homes varied greatly depending on whether these were located in the countryside or in urban areas, not to mention considerations such as family wealth, which set clear limits on material life. There were also regional differences, although the lifestyles of the middle and upper classes were very similar from country to country. The head of the Victorian family was the father, whose role in the patriarchal way of life was that of the 'bread-winner'. He went to work, lunched at the gentlemen's club and then spent the evenings with his family unless entertainment outside the home was in store.[13] His role also required that he act as host and entertain guests in the home. In the novel *Buddenbrooks* which appeared on the threshold of the new century in 1901, Thomas Mann describes the life of the northern German bourgeoisie. Mann's book begins with an account of a grand party. Departing from the dinner table, visitors disperse into the other rooms either to smoke a cigar or partake of the beverages. There is chatter everywhere and music is anticipated:

> They were rising from table.
>
> 'Well, ladies and gentleman, *gesegnete Mahlzeit*! Cigars and coffee in the next room, and a liqueur if Madame feels generous . . . Billiards for whoever chooses. Jean, you will show them the way back to the billiard-room? Madame Köppen, may I have the honour?'
>
> Full of well-being, laughing and chattering, the company trooped back through the folding doors into the landscape-room. The Consul remained behind, and collected about him the gentlemen who wanted to play billiards.
>
> 'You won't try a game, Father?'
>
> No, Lebrecht Kröger would stop with the ladies, but Justus might go if he liked . . . Senator Landhals, Köppen, Gratjens, and Doctor Grabow went with the Consul, and Jean Jacques Hoffstede said he

would join them later. 'Johann Buddenbrook is going to play the flute,' he said. 'I must stop for that. *Au revoir, messieurs.*'

As the gentlemen passed through the hall, they could hear from the landscape-room the first notes of the flute accompanied by the Frau Consul on the harmonium: an airy, charming little melody that floated sweetly through the lofty rooms. The Consul listened as long as he could. He would have liked to stop behind in an easy-chair in the landscape-room and indulge the reveries that the music conjured up; but his duties as host . . .

'Bring some coffee and cigars into the billiard-room,' he said to the maid whom he met in the entry.[14]

The perspective adopted in the *Buddenbrooks* is consciously masculine. The head of the family has tight rein over the merchant family from Lübeck. In the excerpt quoted, Mann juxtaposes the private home – the armchair, where one can let one's self drift into a world of dreams and emotions – and the home as a public space, in which the host has responsibilities. Tearing himself away from the sensory pleasure offered by the home, the host gives instructions to the maid, even though the management of the house is properly the task of the wife. The host Mann portrays appears to be a man well-versed in daily household matters, the nucleus directing the staff, yet the nineteenth-century household was most often managed by the wife. She planned the meals, did the purchases, gave instructions to the servants and visited relations and friends. Lesser, more menial tasks belonged to the servants.[15]

Since labour was inexpensive, the middle-class family generally had at least one maid. Usually there were three employees: in addition to the maid there was a driver and a cook. If the family was wealthy, there might also be a scullery maid, a nanny, a private tutor, a gardener and a butler. The servants took care of manual work, cleaning, dusting and cooking. If there was only one servant, the mistress of the house might also have to dirty her hands.

The nineteenth-century middle-class family lived according to a strict daily rhythm. The mistress was in charge of the schedule and – at least in principle – was the first to get up in the mornings and the last to go to bed at night. In French instructional books for housewives it was deemed appropriate that the mistress of the house woke up at half past six or seven in the summers and an hour later in wintertime. Middle- and upper-class women generally did not go out in the mornings. According to etiquette, women walking outside at inappropriate times were not even to be greeted. Meals were taken at set times during the day. All family members were expected to be present and appropriately dressed. Meal times varied according to whether people lived in the country or in urban areas. There were, of course, significant national and regional differences.

The afternoons of middle- and upper-class households were devoted to social life and responsibilities both within and outside the home. Visiting cards might even state the day of the week and the time of day that the mistress could be found at home. In Paris visitors were received between three and seven in the afternoons and elsewhere in France between two and six. When receiving visitors, the hostess usually sat in the salon to the right of the fireplace. This practice changed in the 1880s and the hostess moved to the middle of the room. She rose up, if the visitor was a clergyman, a woman or an older man; otherwise she received her visitors seated. The salons were furnished with a table where visitors were served cakes and sandwiches. The daughter of the house brought tea. Female visitors usually stayed only briefly since they often had other receptions to go to. An appropriately timed visit lasted from a quarter of an hour to half an hour. Such receptions gradually came to a crisis at the turn of the twentieth century as etiquette bound women more tightly to their homes. The practice disappeared with the First World War.[16]

Temporal patterns were evident in nineteenth-century family life in things other than daily routines, too. Equally important were weekly routines and annual rhythms. Sunday was a holy day which the family spent going to church and enjoying a quiet existence. Religion was still important to nineteenth-century Europeans, although life was more secularized than in previous centuries.[17] The Pietistic movement which emphasized the role of private religious feelings had become common in central Europe by the eighteenth century. These revivalist movements spread to the rest of Europe during the nineteenth century but did little to disturb the regularity of middle-class life. Although religious experience was private, observance of practices was still regarded as essential. In the annual calendar, ecclesiastical holidays and festivals played an important role, ordering life just as much as the changing seasons.[18]

As has already become apparent, etiquette played an essential practical role in the lives of the middle and upper classes. The rules of propriety were detailed and strict, and no one was exempted. If boundaries were crossed the community might completely ignore the one who had acted immorally or otherwise breached the rules. The world of set schedules and temporal rhythms introduced above had a significant role in the observance of etiquette. The regularity of activities was part of etiquette. Doing the wrong thing at the wrong time was inappropriate. At the same time, regularity thus strengthened customs. Repeated over and over, the social rituals ensured that etiquette remained in active memory. The emphasis on propriety of course turned family life to some extent into a public activity. Although the home was a private sphere, it was also a show window to the outside world, a sign that all was well within the family and that life was decent and respectable.[19]

Without question, home life differed greatly depending on whether a family lived in the country or in cities. As a counterweight to etiquette, middle- and upper-class lifestyles were plagued by an enormous yearning for the countryside, for conditions that appeared, at least, to provide more freedom. If a family was wealthy, it also owned a country residence for spending the summers. With the coming of spring, the family would move to the country.[20] If the summer residence was sufficiently close to the home, the head of the household would commute to work, although he might also stay in the city. The holiday brought a breath of fresh air from beyond the stifling norms and etiquette since the new environment offered the opportunity of encountering new people and unfamiliar situations.[21] Although spending the summer in the country looks like simple migration, it had an important impact on emotional life as well as on conceptions of the environment and surroundings. In addition to staying at their summer residences, middle-class holidaymakers spent a great deal of time at coastal resorts and, later, at more distant tourist attractions. During the nineteenth century, packaged tours increased steadily so that at the turn of the century particularly British travellers could extend their movements even to the furthest reaches of the Empire.[22]

There was obviously a liberating sensuality attached to nature and summertime in bourgeois sensibility that allowed a temporary release from the shackles of etiquette. This is brought out well in Guy de Maupassant's 'A Day in the Country'. In it, Maupassant describes a family's outing away from Paris, to the peace and calm of nature. The trip is timed to coincide with the birthday of iron-monger Dufour's wife, which in itself reflects well the nineteenth-century middle-class customs: birthdays and namedays as well as country outings had their place in the lives of the bourgeoisie. The short story begins with a depiction of the cart ride that gradually takes the party ever further from Paris:

> For five months now they had been planning to have lunch somewhere in the country just outside Paris on the birthday of Madame Dufour, whose name was Pétronille. And because they were looking forward to the outing with some impatience, everyone was up early on the big day.
>
> Monsieur Dufour had borrowed the milkman's cart, and took the reins himself. The vehicle had two wheels and was spotless; it had an awning supported by four iron stanchions to which flaps were attached. They were rolled up so that the occupants could see out as they rode along. The flap at the back hung down loosely and fluttered in the wind like a flag. Madame Dufour, seated next to her husband, was radiant in an extraordinary cerise silk dress. Behind them an aged grandma and a young girl sat on separate seats. Just visible was the flaxen hair of a young man who, since there was nothing for him to sit on, had stretched out on the floor, so that only his head could be seen.
>
> After driving up the avenue of the Champs-Elysées and negotiating the fortifications at the Porte Maillot, everyone had started the gazing at the passing scene. When they reached the bridge at Neuilly, Monsieur Dufour said: 'Ah! The country – at last!' and his wife, on hearing this signal, went into raptures about nature. At the roundabout at Courbevoie, they had been gripped by astonishment on observing how far away the horizon was. Over there, to the right, was Argenteuil with its spire erect; above and beyond loomed the Sannois hills and the mill at Orgement. On their left, the Marly aqueduct stood out against the clear morning sky, and in the distance they could even see the terrace at Saint-Germain. Meanwhile, straight ahead, at the end of a line of hills, recent excavations marked the new fort at Cormeilles. In

the far distance, amazingly far off, beyond the plains and villages, they could make out the dark green of forests.[23]

In this ironic story, Maupassant intentionally sets bourgeois values in opposition to fantasies about nature. Madame Dufour is the prisoner of her own norms, 'laced too tightly', yet in the sensual peace of the countryside she experiences her body more powerfully than ever before. Maupassant recounts how she enjoys the 'thrilling movement' of the swing; she feels dizzy, is frightened and squeals shrilly. In the restaurant, the family meet two athletic rowers to whom both mother and daughter are mysteriously, sexually drawn. In the end, the youths tempt the women to go rowing on the lake and the bounds of etiquette are crossed. In Maupassant's description, bourgeois life is one of alienation. For the daughter, the romantic moment in the shaded forest becomes a lifelong object of longing, an expression of natural intimacy that is not possible anywhere else in her world of strict norms. In the last scene of the story she is described as a married woman for whom the encounter in nature has become a memory.

Maupassant's story is both sarcastic and nostalgic. Excursions like the one it describes were, however, an integral part of the bourgeois lifestyle, as was the romantic mystification of nature it expresses. For the middle-class residents of cities, the countryside and nature became an idealization that was both languorously tempting and fiercely frightening. The mystification of the countryside is also exemplified in Alexander Pushkin's short story 'An Amateur Peasant Girl', which appeared in 1830, almost half a century before Maupassant's story. In it, as in his other work, Pushkin portrays the lifestyles of soldiers and nobility. Seen through the mirror of Russian literature, the role of rural aristocracy is visibly emphasized, yet the perspective in Pushkin's story is clearly urban. He idealizes the inhabitants of the countryside, describing a noble maiden amusing herself by dressing up as a peasant girl:

Those of my readers who have never lived in the country, cannot imagine how charming these provincial young ladies are! Brought up in the pure air, under the shadow of their own apple trees, they derive their knowledge of the world and of life from books. Solitude, freedom, and reading develop very early within them sentiments and passions unknown to our town-bred beauties. For the young ladies of the country the sound of harness bells is an event; a journey to the nearest town marks an epoch in their lives, and the visit of a guest leaves behind a long and sometimes an everlasting memory.[24]

In Pushkin's tale, country maids dwell in romantic fantasies that they glean from the magical world of literature. Like outings, reading played a central part in the lives of the middle and upper classes during the nineteenth century – even though many prejudices were associated with this pastime as demonstrated by the excerpt from Pushkin's story. In a world tightly governed by norms, men as well as women could feed their imaginations through reading the newspapers and literature. Such texts provided a channel for learning as well as for emotional stimulation. It could well be that literature indeed became the main source of life experience for many in a strictly regulated world.

In the short story 'An Amateur Peasant Girl', the cultivation of feelings and passions with the help of literature is something that is linked specifically to young women. This view was widely accepted by the nineteenth century: 200 years earlier, the alienating effect of literature could be symbolized by a character like Don Quijote. The issue came to be seen in terms of gender at the end of the eighteenth century, when the desire to read inspired by popular literature was seen as unhealthy. In Germany this desire to read was called *Lesewut* or *Lesesucht*. The groups that were most at risk of compulsive reading were seen to be women who ravenously consumed literature, especially novels.[25] The consumption of books had expanded as a consequence of increased literacy and the growing numbers of imprints taken, as well as the spread of libraries. Perhaps the best-known portrayal of such harmful reading is to be found in Gustave Flaubert's (1821–80) novel *Madame Bovary* (1857). In this desperate relationship drama, Charles Bovary's wife Emma plunges into the world of novels, causing concern in both husband and mother-in-law:

– Do you know what your wife needs? said Madame Bovary senior. She needs some hard work, some manual labour. If she were like nearly everyone else, forced to earn a living, she wouldn't have these vapours of hers, which all come from stuffing her head with nonsense and leading a life of idleness.

– But she is always busy, said Charles.

– Ah! Busy indeed! And with what? Busy reading novels, wicked books, things written against religion where priests are made a mockery with speeches taken from Voltaire. It all leads to no good, my poor boy, and anyone with no religion always comes to a bad end.

Therefore, it was decided to prevent Emma from reading novels. This was by no means an easy matter. The old lady took it upon herself: on her way through Rouen she was to call in person at the lending library and notify them that Emma was cancelling her subscription. Would they not have the right to tell the police, if the librarian still persisted in his poisonous trade?[26]

Their attempts to keep Emma from her passionate pastime fail. In Flaubert's tale, Emma continuously finds new romantic dreams to feed her fantasies but becomes side-tracked when attempting to realize them. This results in moral decay, the tragic opposite of her dreams. Although Flaubert's *Madame Bovary* does not present reading as an illness in the fashion of the late eighteenth century, it certainly reveals the dangers of escapist daydreaming. As a matter of fact, Flaubert's book played an important role in generating debate concerning escapism and the retreat from reality offered by entertainment. While the concept of escapism itself surfaced later, in the British literary research of the 1930s, the immorality of light entertainment was certainly already a significant issue in the nineteenth century. Unrealistic fantasies were seen as the seed that gradually led those who indulged in them to come into conflict with social norms. In a way, this attitude provided a starting point for the emerging moralism against other forms of entertainment such as the circus, variety theatre and moving pictures at the end of the nineteenth and in the early twentieth centuries. Women and children were perceived as being particularly threatened since light entertainment was thought capable of making them uncritical and passive. In addition, these cultural products – perceived to be of inferior quality – were regarded as fostering immoral attitudes.[27]

The prevalent attitude towards reading in the nineteenth century thus contained a striking double standard. Even research ignored the fact that reading can never be completely passive. It involves an interactive process providing room for creative expression. As a matter of fact, it was due to the general enthusiasm for reading that women also found opportunities for making a career of writing. The novels of Jane Austen (1775–1817) and the Brontë sisters in England, or Conceptión Arenal (1820–93) and Emilia Pardo Bazán (1851–1921) in Spain, demonstrate exactly this kind of creativity. In many other countries, the early stages of prose writing were also more feminine than is generally believed. In both Finland and Sweden many early novelists were women. The gendered view of literature – as well as the underrated position of the novel – is extremely well demonstrated by the fates of Johan Ludvig Runeberg's (1804–77) and Frederika Runeberg's (1807–79) respective oeuvres. The husband of this literary couple became the national poet of Finland while the wife, who wrote novels, had to wait a long time to be discovered by interested researchers.

While women's voluntary and absorbed reading was moralized and questioned, there were, of course, respectable objects for reading. The reading of literature out loud was a normal part of a middle-class family's nightly routines, the head of the household generally doing the reading. In her diaries, Cosima Wagner, for example, tells of such literary entertainment in the evenings. In the home of Richard and Cosima Wagner a great amount of literary fiction, philosophical classics, topical polemics and non-fiction – and of course their own works – was read during the 1860s and the 1870s. The reader was almost always Richard, around whom the family would gather to listen.[28] Maybe the Wagner family cannot be taken as representative of the typical middle-class home since artistic ambitions were in the forefront. Most families would have the Bible read out and its stories would be returned to every once in a while. In any case, reading aloud was part of the family idyll in the nineteenth century. Serial stories in literary magazines and newspapers also offered excellent material. This, in fact, was the form in which many classic novels of the nineteenth century were initially conceived.

There were, of course, popular forms of evening entertainment other than reading. Playing music among the family was another central form of entertainment. The ability to play the piano was regarded as important especially in the education of girls.[29] Indeed, home music formed one of the most significant areas of the musical culture of the nineteenth century, and the manufacture and sale of pianos grew explosively as early as the 1830s and 1840s. At the same time, more and more simplified arrangements of well-known melodies and new tunes were produced. The publishing of musical scores became an important part of the music business. Sales lists were headed primarily by two- and four-handed arrangements made of, for example, well-known operas. Home music retained its strong position until the First World War, after which it was displaced by the rapid spread of the gramophone.[30]

The middle–class family could go to the theatre though the bourgeoisie particularly favoured the opera.[31] In the early nineteenth century, Parisian boulevard theatres became the place for the middle and upper classes to make their appearance, and here the opera offered a grandiose setting for social parlour games. The best-known and most successful opera composer of the time was Giacomo Meyerbeer, whose works such as *The Huguenots*, *The Prophet* and *The African* furnished audiences with virtuoso numbers to delight the ears and extravagant spectacles to please the eye.[32] It is revealing that the stands were fully lit in Parisian opera houses until the 1860s when Wagner dared to darken the hall for the performance of *Tannhäuser* in 1861, the performance becoming a famous fiasco. It was an integral part of opera-going that the audience could observe each other during the performance, show off new clothing and flirt.

Another important social ritual was provided by the balls, in which participation followed strict rules of propriety. Usually balls involved group dances, although the waltz also found its place despite the scandal caused by its physicalness since the end of the previous century. As late as 1857, Gustave Flaubert was made to appear before a court after having depicted the waltz in *Madame Bovary* without hiding its sexual dimension:

> They began slowly, and went faster. They were turning: everything was turning around them, the lamps, the furniture, the panelling, the parquet floor, like a disc on a spindle. Passing near the doors, Emma's

dress, at the hem, caught on his trousers; their legs entwined; he looked down at her, she looked up at him; a lethargy came over her, she stopped. They set off again; and, quickening the pace, the Viscount, pulling her along, disappeared with her to the end of the gallery, where, panting for breath, she almost fell, and, for a moment, rested her head upon his chest. And then, still spinning round, but more slowly, he conducted her back to her seat; she slumped against the wall and put her hand over her eyes.

When she opened them again, in the middle of the room, there was a lady sitting on the stool with three gentlemen kneeling before her. She chose the Viscount, and the violin began to play.

Every eye was on them. Round and round the room they went, she holding herself erect with head down, and he in his fixed pose, shoulders back, arm curved, chin held high. She could certainly waltz, that woman! They carried on for ages and exhausted everyone else.[33]

In middle- and upper-class balls the quadrille and other group dances were preferred to the waltz. Both the waltz and the polka, the fad dance form of the 1840s and 1850s, were associated with a certain vulgarity. Even in group dances, however, the dizziness brought on by dancing offered a hint of a sensual physicality, otherwise frowned upon by Victorian culture. In Flaubert's description of the waltz, the dance gives Emma an inkling of the world beyond the norms. In the end, however, she covers her eyes with her hands: physicality is associated with shame.

An extremely strict sexual morality, which was only further emphasized by religious thinking, prevailed among the middle class.[34] In contrast, sexuality was viewed more openly by the working classes. This in itself was enough to evoke fear in the middle and upper classes. An image of a virile lower class with no bounds to its proliferation emerged. The patriarchal system, in which a man's power was unquestioned, dominated the thinking of all classes. There were, however, cracks in the system that seem to have been building up towards the end of the century. These included phenomena such as the establishment of women's organizations, improvements in the education of women, the beginning of the battle for enfranchisement and a marked increase in the number of women working. Genteel women found a means to independent lives, either in artistic pursuits or through participation in organizations. While it was inappropriate for middle- and upper-class women to work for a living, voluntary work provided many opportunities. Differences inside the middle class were, of course, great. In Finland, for example, where women from the upper middle class could not leave the home to work, more and more lower-middle-class women became civil servants, such as teachers, postmistresses, clerks and nurses. Their occupational status was, however, lower than that of lower-middle-class men.[35] In any event, the turn of the century saw the beginning of a process in which the relations between men and women were redefined and renegotiated, even if the more powerful transformation was to occur only in the aftermath of the First World War.

6

Baudelaire in the Department Store: Urban Living and Consumption

> It is not given to every man to take a bath of multitude; enjoying a crowd is an art; and only he can relish a debauch of vitality at the expense of the human species, on whom, in his cradle, a fairy has bestowed the love of masks and masquerading, the hate of home, and the passion for roaming.[1]

So wrote the French poet Charles Baudelaire in his prose poem 'Crowds', which appeared in the collection *Paris Spleen* (*Le Spleen de Paris*) in 1869.[2] For Baudelaire, 'bathing in the multitude' was part of being urban, of roaming in a metropolis such as Paris. The rupture in urban culture was quite striking for people at the time; they were controlled by the public space and only those who – as the poet says – felt a liking for 'masks and masquerading' could blend in with the urban role-play. Baudelaire's feelings were mixed: occasionally he praised the crowds and the anonymity of the masses in the cities; on other occasions he yearned for solitude, which could ultimately only be found in 'one's own silence'. In the prose poem 'One O'Clock in the Morning', he writes:

> At last! I am alone! Nothing can be heard but the rumbling of a few belated and weary cabs. For a few hours at least silence will be ours, if

not sleep. At last! The tyranny of the human face has disappeared, and now there will be no one but myself to make me suffer.[3]

The city quietens down at night, but never offers rest. Peace can be found only where one is not visible to others, hidden from the merciless spotlight of urban space. Charles Baudelaire's writings have often been taken as a crystallization of modern urban experience. The change was undoubtedly a tangible one: it involved the rearticulation of the relation between the individual and society as well as between private and public space, and it brought out the oppositeness of cities and countryside. Behind these mental changes was an extensive process of social development, the rapid urbanization during the nineteenth century.

Although urbanization in Europe had its roots in the Middle Ages, real growth only began in the wake of industrialization in the nineteenth century. Waged labour tempted increasing numbers of people from the countryside to the urban areas. This internal migration does not, however, alone explain the powerful changes that took place within cities in the course of the century. There was, namely, a great growth in overall population at the same time. According to estimates, there were around 200 million people living in Europe at the start of the nineteenth century, compared to 430 million only a century later. This increase was also significant on a global scale, emphasizing Europe's supremacy. While Asians numbered two thirds of the world's entire population in 1800, they only constituted half by the beginning of the nineteenth century. It should be noted, however, that at the beginning of European industrialization before 1850, the population increased especially in areas that were already rather densely populated. Most of the northern, eastern and Mediterranean parts of the continent experienced their population growth later. Thus, even though urbanization and population growth did happen in the nineteenth century, rural life dominated Europe, and the Baudelairean experiences remained rather remote to the majority of Europeans.[4]

The speed of urbanization varied greatly, being greatest in England and western Europe. In 1851, over half of the populations of Germany and England were already living in urban areas. Urbanization intensified most furiously during the last decades of the century. The population of Berlin, for example, more than doubled between 1871 and 1905, rising to well over two million. Life in the large European cities – London, Paris, Berlin, Rome or St Petersburg – was completely different from that of the country-side or smaller urban centres. The multitudes could be experienced as a chaotic and vague 'crowd' as Baudelaire's texts reveal. In this 'tyranny of the human face', individuality could well be threat-ened. We should, however, keep in mind that there were major differences between cities, and experiences of urban centres like Paris or Berlin cannot be taken to represent all urban experiences. Many features of urban culture that only became stronger during the twentieth century and that we still recognize today originated in the nineteenth-century metropolis.

With accelerating urbanization, everyday life in major cities began to reflect an increasing need to stand out, to demonstrate one's individuality. In a situation where, for purely practical reasons, it was necessary to introduce norms and standards for the handling of daily affairs, individuality was felt to be under threat. The identity of the modern individual was no longer constructed in relation to the family, kin or class but in relation to the urban multitude, the crowd. Dandyism, an aspect of early-nineteenth-century male culture in which one's distinctive dress and behaviour became important in the construction of social and sexual identity, can well be linked to attempts to distinguish oneself from the masses. One of the best-known dandies was the English Beau Brummell (1778–1840), an intimate of the Prince of Wales, char-acterized as the gentleman who defined London's fashion at the time. On 7 January 1830, *The Times* wrote in an ironic manner: 'It is said that Brummell has educated more tailors than any other man of fashion ever ruined.'[5] The poet Lord Byron, too, caused havoc among his contemporaries by dressing in open opposition to the prevailing conventions of the time.[6]

The English dandies were known throughout Europe. They were early representatives of stardom, a media phenomenon just as much as virtuosos like Niccolò Paganini and Franz Liszt. It is revealing of the extent of the publicity that even the Nordic news-papers reported author Edward Bulwer-Lytton's (1803–73) dis-tinctive attire. Bulwer-Lytton was a politician and held, at one time, a cabinet post as Colonial Secretary, yet he is best remembered for his historical novels like *The Last Days of Pompeii* (1834) and *Rienzi* (1835). Throughout Europe, the newspapers reported the wonder that Bulwer-Lytton caused, dressing occasionally completely in white and occasionally completely in black.[7] Another well-known dandy was author Oscar Wilde (1856–1900) whose aestheticized and extravagant lifestyle was perceived as scandalous not only in England but also on the continent.[8] An ambiguous sexual identity was connected to the dandyism of both Lord Byron and Oscar Wilde, and their eccentric clothing and manners were taken as part of its expression.[9] To an extent, dandyism contained the seeds of an intentional exaggeration and camp-sentiment which later became an integral part of gay culture. In Oscar Wilde's case, his sexual identity ultimately became the basis for public persecution and humiliation. In 1895 he was sentenced to hard labour for two counts of 'gross indecency', engaging in homosexual practices, and he spent his remaining years in Paris under the pseudonym Sebastian Melmoth.[10] While the publicity offered by the metropolis, London, provided the building blocks for his dandyism, it was paradoxically another metropolis, Paris, that offered him the opportunity to escape, to disappear from the public eye. Perhaps Wilde's case reflects the dichotomy of urban living, both its mercilessness and its compassion.

Although dandyism involved an intentional construction of identity, it was based on publicity, on being the object of seeing. At the same time, the dandies themselves controlled with their gaze: they were usually social lions, accustomed to moving in salons as much as on the boulevards. In France, the parallel term of *flâneur* was coined and used by contemporaries as early as the 1830s quite like that of the 'dandy'. In his *Passagen-Werk* Walter Benjamin has taken Charles Baudelaire as epitomizing the Parisian *flâneur*.[11] Baudelaire's work, above all his collections of poetry *The Flowers of Evil* (*Les Fleurs du Mal*, 1857) and *Paris Spleen*, build on the sensory experiences and observations to be had in the urban milieu. As Benjamin writes, the *flâneur* strolled along 'studying the cement': he drifted through urban space gripped by a modern sense of fragmentation, searching for refuge from his loneliness in crowded public places, in arcades framed by display windows as well as on the streets and in cafes. In *The Flowers of Evil*, Baudelaire describes the symbiosis of consumption and urban living in the following way:

> Your eyes, lit up like shops to lure their trade . . .
> Or fireworks in the park on holidays,
> insolently make use of borrowed power
> and never learn (you might say, 'in the dark')
> what law it is that governs their good looks.[12]

In 1860 Baudelaire wrote 'The Painter of Modern Life', his essay on Constantin Guys in which he claims: 'His passion and his profession is to merge with the crowd (. . .) He gazes at the landscape of the great city, landscapes of stone, now swathed in the mist, now struck in full face by the sun.'[13] Baudelaire, too, wanted to be a 'perfect idler' and a 'passionate observer' who makes 'the flow of life move by, majestic and dazzling'.[14] The *flâneur* is thus 'wedded to the crowd', searching for crowded places while making observations alone and hoping to reach the transitoriness of modern life. As Baudelaire's essay on Guys indicates, this was primarily an aesthetic ideal concerning the identity of the modern artist. Perhaps the *flâneur* already contained the seeds of the urban dweller who is conscious of the implications of public space. The role of the gaze is greatly emphasized in city space simply because the urban environment requires people to act on the basis of visual information. The 'tyranny of the human face' that Baudelaire mentions in *Paris Spleen* expressly refers to the power of the gaze. The gaze can be used to dominate and to humiliate, to convey messages, to communicate. At the same time the gaze can also be directed: focal points for looking were consciously created in urban areas to draw the attention of the inhabitants (memorials, public buildings, advertisements, posters). The increased significance of dressing and fashion in the major European cities in the nineteenth century can also be attributed to addressing the gaze. The metropolises, especially Paris, became centres of fashion from which innovations quickly spread.

Visual experience of the cities in the nineteenth century was greatly affected by the history of artificial lighting. Originally, lighting was undoubtedly a social issue since the darkness of the cities posed a threat to the residents and to the authorities. The night could hide both criminals and revolutionaries. London received its first gaslights in 1808. In Paris, the revolutions of 1830 and 1848 gave the impetus for the breakthrough of artificial lighting. Since darkness was seen to offer too good a cover for revolutionary forces, light was a means to govern. Following the February revolution in 1848, arc-lamps were installed in Paris to light the streets with an artificial theatricality. The electric lightbulbs developed by Thomas A. Edison only came into widespread use in the last decades of the century. In Berlin this happened in 1882. It is interesting to note that the electric night, the use of artificial lighting in public spaces, lent a theatrical flavour to urban living: going out or *flâneur*-ing resembled the stage performance of a role. Increasingly stronger evaluations also came to be attached to light. Core areas of a city would be brightly lit whereas the suspect lifestyles of the fringes were characterized with symbols of half-light. The objects and areas important to the public image received light whereas those it preferred to be forgotten were left in the dark.[15]

It was on such a stage of light and shade that a *flâneur* like Charles Baudelaire lived his life. In his poetry, Baudelaire also displayed the discomfort that came with continuous presence. With everything visible and on show, modern life inevitably became a masquerade, an interplay of public and private roles. Baudelaire's cityscape could be summarized by the closing poem of *Paris Spleen*:

> Happy of heart I climbed the hill
> To contemplate the town in its enormity,
> Brothel and hospital, prison, purgatory, hell,
>
> Monstrosities flowering like a flower.
> But you, O Satan, patron of my pain,
> Know I went not to weep for them in vain.
>
> But like old lecher to old mistress goes,
> Seeking but rapture, I sought out this trull
> Immense, whose hellish charm resuscitates.

> Whether in morning sheets you lie asleep,
> Hidden and heavy with a cold, or flaunt
> Through night in golden spangled veils,
>
> Infamous City, I adore you! Courtesans
> And bandits, you offer me such joys,
> The common herd can never understand.[16]

Baudelaire's mythical Paris is simultaneously a hospital, a purgatory and a prison. There is no escape from it yet it is the only thing that can bring salvation. The picture is conflicting. The city wavers in the interim between coldness and heat, Satan and piety, old age and youth, enjoyment and suffering, anger and love. Another captivating dilemma is in the attitude to crowds, the multitude. Although the aim of the *flâneur* is to be 'wedded to the crowds', Baudelaire ends his poem with the claim that the foolish masses fail to appreciate the 'courtesans and bandits' that 'offer me such joys'. For the poet, the city could hardly exist without its contradictions, indeed: oppositions are an essential part of what the city is. The modern metropolis is simultaneously holy and depraved.

It is striking that, in Baudelaire's vision, the city is portrayed as female. The *flâneur*'s point of view is clearly male. The wandering eye, domination through looking, as well as being seen, are all expressly marked as masculine. An interesting question to be asked regarding urban space in the nineteenth century is that of how the city also became a stage for displaying gender. In part at least, this must have been associated with the process of social change that led to the severing of traditional family ties in industrial society. In the artificial environment of the cities the mechanisms for the construction and definition of identities also had to change.

Rapid urbanization, the expansion of the monetary economy and the transformation of urban space altered the nature of publicity. This meant that the role of women in public life could also change. In her book *Window Shopping* (1993), the American media scholar Anne Friedberg has claimed that in addition to the male *flâneur*, the cityscape offered a place for the *flâneuse*, the female wanderer and spectator.[17] We must bear in mind that there were, after all, relatively few public spaces in the nineteenth century that women had access to. Towards the end of the century these included arcades and department stores, and finally also cinemas. According to Friedberg, the history of the *flâneuse* is linked to the rise of consumer culture. It was in particular the department store that, with its visual attractions, became the ultimate refuge for the wandering spectator. The gaze changed into the consuming look, a means for acquiring material pleasure and feeding lavish fantasies.[18]

The larger department stores were born in the mid-nineteenth century. Bon Marché opened its doors in Paris in 1852; Macy's in New York in 1857. These emporiums were a sign of the strong economic boom of the cities and the consequent increase in affluence. The author Émile Zola has depicted the desires awakened by department stores in his novel *The Ladies' Paradise* (*Au bonheur des dames*, 1883), which portrays women as particular targets of consumer fantasies. The novel describes the transformation in young Denise, who comes to Paris from the rural town of Valognes. The novel begins with a scene where she is walking from the railway station of Saint-Lazare towards the centre of the busy metropolis, when she abruptly freezes in front of the shop windows of Bonheur des Dames.

Denise is stopped, above all, by the display windows, in which products have been transformed into visual attractions. According to Zola, the department store appealed not only to Denise but to all classes of women who were captured by the tempting pleasure.[19] In his harsh condemnation of consumer culture, Zola compares the department store to a machine that functions with methodical accuracy and is 'lubricated' by women, those feminine consumer fantasies. The owner of the store, a Monsieur Mouret, intentionally has clothes and luxury goods displayed in such a fashion that they would produce a maximal hypnotic effect on passing women. Zola writes:

> Mouret's unique passion was to conquer woman. He wished her to be queen in his house, and he had built this temple to get her completely at his mercy. His sole aim was to intoxicate her with gallant attentions, and traffic on her desires, work on her fever.[20]

Mouret's desire to induce a lust for consumption reaches almost pathologic proportions. Zola depicts women's behaviour as being equally governed by drives. He compares the desire provoked by display windows to hypnosis, a dream that transforms the consumer into an unwitting victim of promotion. Zola's interpretation is powerful and polemic. Although Zola's work is often labelled as naturalist, *Ladies' Paradise* is far from being a realist description of the consumer hysteria surfacing at the end of the nineteenth century. Taking a critical view of entrepreneurs as well as the consumers who allow themselves to be turned into passive objects waiting to be seduced, the author presents a passionate agenda of his own. Zola's description can easily be viewed in context of the tradition in which women were presented as easily succumbing to the temptations of light entertainment. As noted in the previous chapter, descriptions of a lust for reading that led readers to rush into the fantasy lives depicted in novels with reckless abandon can be found already in eighteenth-century Germany. The same moralizing attitude was reflected in Gustave Flaubert's *Madame Bovary*, in which the protagonist living in the false world of popular literature was incapable of distinguishing between reality and fantasy. On Flaubert's view, the dangers of Bovarism threatened especially women who, through popular entertainment, became passive and dependent. It is significant that an almost identical debate was going on at the beginning of the twentieth century. In Germany *Kinosucht*, a lust for the cinema, was seen to bring a danger that both women and children could easily fall prey to.[21] In a way, Zola's portrayal of women as consumers belongs to this tradition. Attention focused on women as consumers of material culture just as it did on them as consumers of popular entertainment.

Although Zola's description is exaggerated, a concrete change in consumer culture is reflected in *The Ladies' Paradise*. Large department stores began hiring more female sales staff and thus made it possible for women to be both employees and customers, something that had not been as self-evident earlier. This marked a significant change in women's public lives. As Anne Friedberg points out, towards the end of the century the department store became an oasis or haven for the mobile urban woman, a place where she could move without a chaperone.[22] On the other hand, these changes also created the stereotype of women as consumers, the idea that window shopping or shopping was an

especially feminine characteristic. Like gender roles more generally, this view too is culturally constructed. It is clear that consumption has been important in defining identity in male culture
as well; the history of male shopping has, however, not yet been
written.

With the emergence of consumer culture at the end of the
nineteenth century, advertising gained a more important role in
the urban environment. Newspaper advertisements and posters
became an integral part of the street scene. Addressing potential
consumers through words and images, and dividing the public into
target groups, together with the general development of advertising strategies, progressed at a furious pace. The first guidebooks on
the subject – aimed at sharpening the advertising rhetoric used in
the business world – appeared.

In Europe, the growth of consumption continued until the First
World War. In addition to bringing satisfaction, shopping – the
acquisition of products – became a means for the construction of
identity. Self-understanding was built through consumption. This
development was part of the process that gradually wiped out all
traces of the old class society.

Naturally, the rise of consumerism is linked to money, the circulation of which kept accelerating. Imperialist culture played its
part in strengthening this circulation, since the raw materials that
flowed to Europe from other continents enabled rapid economic
growth. The end of the nineteenth century was indeed a golden
age for banks, insurance companies and big business. It is not surprising, then, that at the turn of the century Georg Simmel was to
contemplate the deeper issues involved with money in his
Philosophy of Money (*Philosophie des Geldes*, 1900):

> There are a large number of occupations in modern cities, such as
> certain categories of general and trading agents and all those indeter-
> minate forms of livelihood in large cities, which do not have any objec-
> tive form and decisiveness of activity. For such people, economic life,
> the web of their teleological series, has no definite content for them
> except making money. Money, the absolutely entity, is for them the
> fixed point around which their activity circulates with unlimited
> scope.[23]

The fact that the economy no longer had any clear objective other than that of making money speaks of a cynical view of life. During the last decades of the nineteenth century, the emergence of consumerism was one of the factors giving rise to pessimistic views concerning the future of the western world. At the centre of it all was 'money, the absolutely entity'.

7

The Breakthrough of Mechanical Reproduction

Those who took up cinematography all began by making natural views . . . views taken in the streets, in the squares, by the sea, on river-banks, in boats, on trains; panoramic views, ceremonies, parades, funeral processions, etc. . . . After at first taking very simple subjects, astonishing solely because of the novelty of movement in photographic prints which had always been frozen and immobile, cameramen today, by travelling throughout the entire world, present extremely interesting spectacles that we can watch without putting ourselves out. They show us countries that we probably have not seen, along with their costumes, animals, streets, inhabitants, and customs – all rendered with a photographic fidelity. The landscapes of India, Canada, Algeria, China, and Russia, the waterfalls, the snow-covered countries and their sports, the misty or sun-drenched regions, everything has been filmed for the pleasure of people who do not like to put themselves out.[1]

This is how Georges Méliès, a French pioneer of early cinema, characterized the possibilities offered by moving pictures in 1907. In Méliès's interpretation, films made the world visible, the viewer could see landscapes that would otherwise have remained unknown. This was, undoubtedly, true. With the breakthrough of early cinema at the end of the nineteenth century, moving pictures transported viewers to the furthest regions of the globe, turning them into *flâneurs* who no longer needed to move among the crowds in the Baudelairean sense – they could simply sit in the darkened cinema. Méliès's text exaggerates, however, in that the process of visualization had already begun sometime earlier. The great sensation from Méliès's point of view was, of course, the fact that the photograph was now in motion.

Developed in the seventeenth century, the magic lantern, the *lanterna magica*, had provided the means to arrange armchair travel with reflected pictures. The public could be shown exotic landscapes, foreign cities, current world events, and the ravages of earthquakes and fires. Slides, like so many other visual effects, were in common use in theatres during the nineteenth century to emphasize the spectacle-like nature of the event. Magic lantern pictures formed shows of their own, in which the pictures could even be made to move by combining them together. Visual attractions had also been available in peep shows (*Guckkasten*) since the seventeenth century; peeking into boxes, viewers of peep shows could look at scenes that were presented in full perspective or even follow dramas.[2] In later centuries, visual toys that were based on peeking were very popular. When the stereoscope was first shown at the Crystal Palace Exhibition in London in 1851, Queen Victoria took a fancy to the apparatus. After the Exhibition, over a quarter of a million stereoscopes were sold in London and Paris alone.[3] By peeking into the implement, the viewer could briefly visit landscapes from the Holy Land, well-known Mediterranean sights, or distant continents.[4]

Although the culture of the image has a centuries-old, complicated and fascinating history, the nineteenth century can be seen as marking a significant turning point in the production of images. The number of images simply exploded after the production of copies became industrialized with the invention of new printing and replicating methods. The circulation of pictures in western culture was especially greatly affected by advances in photography since the 1830s. With the help of a camera obscura, the Frenchman Joseph Nicéphore Niépce had created an elementary photograph on a tin plate as early as 1826. Another pioneer of early photography was Louis Jacques Mandé Daguerre, whose daguerreotypes quickly came to be of commercial significance.[5] When the method was announced in France in August 1839, Daguerre's exhibition of pictures received wide international attention. Professor von Nordman travelled all the way from Finland to Paris to see this exhibition of forty daguerreotypes, noting in amazement that, with the help of a magnifying glass, he was able to read a text on the wall of one of the photographed buildings. He sent a report of what he had seen to the Russian Academy of Sciences in St Petersburg.[6] In Daguerre's technique, the picture was taken on to a copper plate and fixed with a solution of sodium sulphate. The fact that the picture was unique restricted the spread of the daguerreotype. Duplicates for distribution in large editions could not be made from it.

In the following decades, various photographic methods were developed in which either paper or glass plates were exposed. Proper mass production of photographs only began when the Englishman Richard Leach Maddox developed the so-called dry-plate process (1871), in which the negative could be made before-hand and exposed when needed. At the initiative of George Eastman the industrial production of dry-plates began in 1880. This attracted more entrepreneurs to photography, especially as making photographs no longer required exposure to dangerous chemicals.[7] By the last decades of the century, photography was already an inexpensive and quick means for producing pictures. At the same time, new printing techniques made the inclusion of photographs in newspapers possible: the reign of images had begun.

An intriguing question that seems to have remained uninvesti-gated is that of how photography has actually influenced western thought and understanding, especially the image of the self, both as a mental and as a corporeal entity. The French historian Alan Corbin has pointed out that it was precisely during the nineteenth century that the popularity of mirrors – although already in evi-dence earlier – rose to unparalleled proportions. 'Self-reflection' quite concretely became part of the bourgeois lifestyle, and one's own appearance and decency, one's clothing and body, were observed 'through the eyes of others' with the help of mirrors.[8] Photography, similarly, offered the possibility of setting oneself outside one's own body. Visits to the photographer became common in Scandinavia during the 1860s: it was now possible to let oneself be photographed at different phases in life and present images as souvenirs and visiting cards.[9] It can be argued that positioning oneself before the lens had an impact on self-conceptions; individuality became objectified. At the same time, corporeal identity could now be historically extended by means of family albums.

Although photography was mainly used for producing portraits and visiting cards and was thus closely embedded in nineteenth-century customs, the new method was also tied in with the development of popular culture. In fact, Daguerre himself had started his career as an assistant to the panorama painter Pierre Prévost. He had a close connection to the visual arts and their popular application. In 1822 Daguerre publicly displayed a viewing device – the diorama – that noticeably increased the panorama's possibilities of transporting its audience to new environments. Unlike the panorama, the viewer of the diorama remained at the centre of a room and the scenery moved. Indeed, a news commentary from the time reported how 'Parisians, who enjoyed easy pleasures, could travel to Switzerland or England without needing to leave the capital.'[10] The diorama – like so many of its equivalents – offered the spectator the possibility of virtual movement. Armchair travel was a reality long before the actual packaged tours of Thomas Cook or the imaginary cinematic travels extolled by Méliès.

Even if the cinema, as an innovation, did not come out of a vacuum but had a long history at its inception, motion pictures offered movement a whole new set of possibilities. Where the photograph had brought industrial manufacture and mechanical reproduction to the sphere of visual culture, influencing both entertainment and art, the cinema produced and packaged movement, translating it into a reproducible form. Cinema was at once the fruit of the nineteenth century and the seed of the twentieth.

A dichotomy of sorts was central to the development of the cinema: the camera and the projector evolved along two different lines. The original form of the camera was the camera obscura, a dark room, in which an image from outside was projected through a hole in the wall. This invention was employed by the arts and sciences as early as the Renaissance. The origin of the projector, on the other hand, was the magic lantern built by the Dutch physicist Christian Huyghens in the 1650s, which was used to project images drawn on glass. Photographs were first shown with this kind of projector in the 1870s.[11] Magic lanterns were extremely popular throughout the century, and they were used for various educational and entertaining purposes. When David Livingstone journeyed to Africa, he took a lantern with him and, after organizing a show at Gonye Falls on the Zambezi in November 1853, he wrote in his travelogue: 'Here, as elsewhere, all petitioned for the magic lantern; and, as it is a good means of conveying instruction, I willingly complied.'[12]

It is hard to say how the shift from magic lantern to the first movie cameras and projectors happened but undoubtedly there were many inventors and engineers in Europe and in the United States that worked in the field during the 1890s, among them Robert W. Paul and Birt Acres in England, Henri Joly in France, Woodville Latham, Thomas Armat and W. K. L. Dickson in the United States, Filoteo Alberini in Italy, the Skladanowsky brothers in Germany and the Lumière brothers in France. Many features of a centuries-old audio-visual culture contributed to this technical development. Recent research on cinematic history has particularly emphasized the fact that the history of motion pictures cannot be separated from the broader audio-visual backdrop of the nineteenth century.[13] Magic lantern presentations, for example, were extremely popular at the end of the century. For the price of an entrance ticket, projected images were shown in darkened halls, sometimes even accompanied by live music and sound effects. A good demonstration of the popularity of these presentations is to be found in the fact that there were twenty-eight companies producing them in London during the 1880s.[14] It can be argued, then, that when motion picture shows for paying audiences appeared in the 1890s the audience was already accustomed to watching images projected on to a screen in darkened rooms – at least in the major cities. The realism of motion was perhaps new but the social setting was familiar.

The emerging cinema borrowed heavily from the theatre. This did not, however, happen until the appearance of films with storylines at the beginning of the twentieth century. Film found its themes as well as its means of presentation in the bourgeois theatre of the nineteenth century. Melodrama, historical adventure, excitement, war, love and the Wild West were adopted as subjects for films. All in all, the cinema seems to have come about from an assortment of ingredients, various features of the culture of the urban poor and the popular culture of the bourgeoisie. This connection with popular culture led to early cinema being the entertainment of the lower classes. The French film historian George Sadoul has described the audience of the early nickelodeon theatres in the following way:

> Within a few years approximately three thousand little cinemas opened their doors in the United States, receiving their name nickelodeon from the fact that the audience consisted of members of the lower classes who paid five cents for their tickets. Side-by-side with Woolworth's stores, where everything cost a nickel or a dime, these low-priced businesses of the entertainment world grew into theatre chains that extended from the Atlantic to the Pacific.
>
> The audience of the nickelodeons comprised primarily of immigrants who had recently arrived from Europe, most of whom could neither read nor write and only spoke a few words of English. In these little theatres Slovaks and Poles from the Chicago slaughter-houses, Ukrainian furriers who had survived the persecution of Jews by the Czar, Greeks thrown onto the streets of New York by the crisis of 1907, or Puerto Rican dock-workers and large Irish families crammed into the slums of Chicago all tried to find a release from their worries for the price of a beer, one nickel.[15]

Although there were many independent innovators working in the industry at the same time, histories of the early cinema often emphasize the role of the French Lumière brothers. In marketing their moving pictures, the Lumière brothers succeeded best. The history of commercial cinema is often seen to begin in a Parisian cafe on the Boulevard des Capucines where, on 28 December 1895, the brothers held a screening which included, for example, the movies *Workers Leaving the Lumière Factory*, *The Sprinkler Sprinkled* and *Baby's Meal*. The Lumière brothers established the first business enterprise of the motion picture industry and also brought the miracle of moving pictures to the remotest corners of Europe. On these travels, the cameramen employed by the brothers filmed new movies, further adding to the appeal of cinematic journeys around the world: the world was on the silver screen. In Helsinki in Finland, the first films were seen in June 1896, only half a year after the Paris premiere. On the eve of the Finnish premiere, the newspaper *Uusi Suometar* wrote:

> The presenter of the Cinématographe Lumière had invited journalists to the hall of the Seurahuone yesterday evening to see the miraculous machine. It is not without reason that he calls this apparatus a nineteenth-century miracle in his announcement; it is, indeed, amazing. It conjures onto a tautly stretched white canvas living photographs that move and act quite naturally. The first picture we saw last night showed the arrival of a railway train to the station of a large city. Why, the life and bustle in it! From afar, the arrival of the train could be perceived and it approached so naturally that we almost feared being run over. It stopped in time, however, and the doors of the carriages opened and passengers with their luggage flooded out to shake hands and converse with waiting relatives and acquaintances. It all happened so naturally that we were quite dumbfounded. Another picture showed two children having a quarrel over their toys. Most striking in this picture was the infinite clarity of the expressions on their faces. Apart from these, the canvas revealed a smithy, in which two men were working. The flying sparks, the smoke, as well as many of the phenomena to be found in the forge were absolutely magnificent.[16]

The journalist for the *Uusi Suometar* refers to the Lumière brothers' film *The Train Arrives at the Station*, saying that the members of the press 'almost feared being run over'. A similar story is in fact told of the brothers' premiere in Paris. It was claimed that the audience climbed on to their chairs, fearing the train that seemed to be puffing from the screen into the stands. The story has been repeated in connection with experiences of other early films also, but no assurance of its truthfulness is available. Even Robert W. Paul refers to the assumed event in his film *The Countryman and the Cinematograph* (1901), in which a simple rural man is unable to distinguish between 'reality' and 'film'.[17] The myth of fear seems to have arisen simply to portray the innocence of cinema audiences at the end of the nineteenth century. In Spain, the Lumière brothers' film was shown under the name *La llegada de un tren* and, according to traditional film histories, it terrified Spanish audiences who believed that the train would burst through the screen. In the Spanish context, however, the audience's reaction has been interpreted as a reflection of the local feeling of backwardness and anxiety in the face of the pressures of modern technological culture.[18]

Film historian Tom Gunning has seen the arrival of the train as a primal scene in film history, not because of its supposed 'reality', but because it has affected the later understanding of how film, and entertainment in general, influences the audience. Since then, film theorists have envisioned 'audiences submitting passively to an all-dominating apparatus, hypnotised and transfixed by its illusionist power'.[19] Gunning argues, however, that the first audiences were not at all as naïve as they have been presented to be: they were sophisticated urban pleasure seekers who were already familiar with optical illusions and other audio-visual attractions of the nineteenth century.[20]

The journalist of *Uusi Suometar* paid attention not only to the shock effects that became a typical feature of early cinema. He also noted the humorous possibilities of the medium, which enriches our view of early film reception:

> Most amusing of all was a man watering a lawn – quite like the one to be found on our esplanade and elsewhere, squirting water from a hose connected to a water pipe. There was really nothing more to this than the fact that the water coming out of the hose looked very natural, but the poor old fool was played quite a prank. A little urchin appeared in the picture and secretly stood on the hose, cutting off the water. The old man wonders, takes his time, and finally turns the hose toward himself hoping to see what the trouble is; at the same time the boy jumps off the hose and the water bursts forcefully on the old man, even throwing his hat clear. The man becomes furious, looks behind himself, sees what the boy has done, runs to catch him and begins to forcefully beat the spot where the back ends. There were also streetscenes of several large cities, in which people, horses, omnibuses, carriages, bicycles, dogs and urchins swarmed *en masse*.

It seems certain that the public of our city cannot restrain themselves from flocking to see this strange machine since the images have been photographed from nature and are shown on the canvas in an amazingly natural manner. According to the announcement, the machine will be shown only today and on Monday. Each must thus quickly hasten to see this amusing spectacle.[21]

The report by the Finnish journalist is interesting in many other respects as well. The author has clearly given a great deal of attention to the 'streetscenes of several large cities' that were portrayed so vividly by the moving pictures. In 1896 Finland was still unquestionably a rural country. Most of the population lived in the country and the number of city dwellers remained small until after the Second World War. In central Europe the situation was different: urbanization proceeded rapidly during the last decades of the century. If moving pictures offered elsewhere the public the opportunity of seeing 'snow-covered countries and their sports', in a country such as Finland, or perhaps Spain too, film seemed to be a product of the new and modern urban culture. It brought the possibility of experiencing the bustle of the metropolis that was not available in the urban centres of the more distant regions. In front of the silver screen, even Finnish viewers could become urban *flâneurs* letting their gaze wander amid the bustle of arcades and markets.

During its first decade, film was transformed from enthusiastic experiments into a large-scale industry. Already in the first decade of the twentieth century film producers had a global market. At the same time, the ambitions of mechanical reproduction centred on sounds, although the combination of images and sound would not occur until after the First World War. Mechanical music had been an area of keen interest in Europe throughout the nineteenth century: automatic pianos, music boxes and other mechanical musical instruments were popular. Although even pianists like Franz Liszt made rolls for the automatic pianos, mechanical music offered no threat to home music or concerts.

A new method was developed by the American inventor Thomas Alva Edison (1847–1931) who shaped modern urban culture in other ways also. Edison's inventions are still to be seen and heard: he participated in the development of the electric lightbulb, the telephone and the microphone, as well as film and sound technology.

In 1877, Edison spoke the very first recorded words (the nursery rhyme 'Mary Had a Little Lamb') into his latest invention. According to *The Times*, 'the public was amazed with the marvels of Mr. Edison's phonograph, a machine whereby articulate speech can be stored up for an unlimited period and given forth at any time at the will of the possessor'.[22] The central part of the phonograph consisted of a steel cylinder wrapped in tinfoil. When someone spoke into the funnel of the phonograph a diaphragm attached to its end vibrated. A needle that followed the movements of the diaphragm simultaneously traced grooves on to the tinfoil that corresponded with the vibrations. After the recording, the needle could be placed at the beginning of the groove and the recorded speech could be heard from the funnel. Edison patented his invention, thinking it might prove useful in many areas of life. He left the phonograph for some time after its invention, returning to it in the 1880s. The phonograph never became a popular household item, although it was sold to universities and wealthy private homes. In 1889 Edison began to systematically manufacture pre-recorded cylinders of music together with the Columbia Phonograph Company. Although the material of the cylinders changed from tinfoil to wax, their replication was still limited, and a single musical performance could not be distributed very widely. In 1896 Edison developed a simpler version of his machine that was more suited to home use but even this ended up selling at the, for the time, relatively high price of forty dollars.[23]

When Edison published his first phonograph in 1877, it quickly became a world sensation. Its inventor was followed 'with feverish anxiety' all over the United States and Europe.[24] Zachris Topelius penned a poem, 'The First Phonograph', in 1878 and predicted a brilliant future for 'echo's rival'. The poem gives an idea of the feelings the machine inspired:

> Fleeting waft,
> The air's fluttering,
> jesting, garrulous
> draught!

A tremulous sigh from nature's lung,
Thou hast been bless'd with a talkative tongue.
Without a thought, of true life shorn,
Thou grindest words from thy monstrous horn.

Be quiet, dearie!
For a time
tame that gravelly,
bleeting, barking
talk of thine!

Thou art still a rooster, crowing with ease,
thy voice breaking hoarsely, in mime of talk;
the day shall come when thou wilt seize
words from the lips with talons of a hawk.

Echo's rival,
thou sound's haunting,
mimicking, flaunting
mirror speech!

The song of the future thou shalt sing,
with many a Midas thy charms adoring . . .
The human voice is universal music,
never to be matched by thy mechanics.[25]

This poem by Topelius reveals the enthusiasm and reservations simultaneously felt for technology's latest achievement. Topelius compares the phonograph to a barrel-organ that produces sound 'without thoughts and life' and that is loud, almost disturbing. The phonograph sings the 'song of the future' and thus points the way for technological development. At the end of the century the future was often depicted as already present through technology. The new device was a symptom of future developments and was interpreted as a starting point of a process that otherwise still remained shrouded.

Topelius's ambiguous attitude is emphasized when he reminds us that artificial, mechanical sound can never replace the human voice. Media technological innovations have often been linked to the idea of the disappearance of creativity or originality. This sentiment appears in Topelius's verse also, even though the 'age of mechanics' would not arrive until the twentieth century. After the turn of the century, a similarity was often observed between media and production technology. Creativity disappeared from the consumption of culture in much the same way as it did from the production process. In relation to the first stages of the phonograph this kind of connection was probably not yet seen.

The fact that the phonograph was known in different corners of Europe as early as 1878 shows clearly how effectively it had entered the public imagination. In addition to publicity by newspapers, touring demonstrations quickly made the new wondrous invention widely known. Phonograph demonstrators travelled diligently from one locality to another. It was not always received with enthusiasm as it seemed noisy and its sound was not very clear. As late as 1904 one listener wrote to the editor of the *Uusi Suometar*, complaining that 'Edison's latest concert machine' plays 'so poorly it makes one's ears ache'.[26]

At the turn of the century the phonograph surprisingly received a rival that in many ways proved to be a more useful household appliance. This device was the gramophone. The Americanized German Jew Emil Berliner had patented the appliance in 1887. Instead of a cylinder, sound in the gramophone was recorded on to a flat disc, in the grooves of which the needle vibrated. From the start, the invention was better suited to the industrial reproduction of recordings than the awkward wax cylinders. It took Berliner a long time to find a suitable material for the recording, but records began to sell from the 1890s onward. By degrees it was learned how to take dies of the original recordings that could be distributed around the world so that the same product could be reproduced in different record factories.[27]

One of the first record companies was the Gramophone Company, founded by William Barry Owen in 1898, which received the rights from Berliner for marketing gramophones and records in Europe. In the 1920s the company coined the trademark 'His Master's Voice'. Branch offices and subsidiaries were quickly born all over Europe.[28] The foundations for the avalanche of mechanical music were thus laid during the last decades of the nineteenth century even if the era of sound recordings did not properly begin until after the First World War. These changes enabled the large-scale production of images and sound that has in many ways characterized European culture during the twentieth century.

This is not to say, however, that methods of mechanical reproduction were not a significant cultural factor in the nineteenth century. The diversification of forms of visual culture was rapid and the circulation of images seemed to increase in step with the improved possibilities and technological advances in transportation. At the same time, technology offered new opportunities in the manipulation of images and opinions. The borderline between real ideas and images was changeable as was tangibly demonstrated by the colonialist culture towards the end of the century. Images and their reproductions were used to shape opinion about other continents and unknown cultures. Anthropology found photography to be an invaluable tool in the recording of ethnic characteristics: the features of foreign races were etched into the European consciousness by a kaleidoscopic stream of photographs and publications.

8

Colonial Culture and European Identity

Although the nineteenth century was a time of rising nationalism, European culture did not only look inward, towards its past or within its 'narrow' geographical boundaries. At the same time as the increase in mobility of information and goods, there was a growing interest in areas beyond the borders of Europe. The German philosopher Georg Wilhelm Friedrich Hegel perceived world history as a dynamic phenomenon at the beginning of the nineteenth century, characterized by movement from the east to the west.[1] History was not stable but, rather, subject to continuous change. The longing for faraway places was symbolized by the sea, which European culture had aspired and would continue to aspire to cross. Over centuries and even millennia, European identity had in fact formed in opposition to others, to surrounding cultures and continents. The cultures of Ancient Greece and Rome emphasized the difference between civilization and barbarity. At times, it was the Persians and at others the Germans who provided the counterpoint and thus essential material for the construction of identity. In the Middle Ages and in early modern times the Arabs and the Turks held a somewhat similar role.

Even though the history of European colonialism is long and its significance since the fifteenth century undeniable, it was in the nineteenth century that colonialist politics saw its heyday. Colonialism was coupled with the parallel concept of imperialism. Behind the concept lies the Latin word *imperium*, power to command. Generally, it is used to refer to the period starting from around the middle of the nineteenth century and ending with the First World War. During that time almost all of Africa and a substantial part of Asia were forced under European dominion.[2] It was not only a matter of political or economic competition. Colonialism can also be understood as a cultural phenomenon that included conceptions and values (opinions about other 'races' and exotic cultures), the production of entertainment and art (literature, photography, painting, music hall, travel accounts, shows) as well as completely new cultural forms (the transformation of travel to distant places into tourism). The colonialist attitude was also visible in the humanities. Archaeological expeditions in the Middle East were largely made possible by political expansion. The effects of colonialism and imperialism also had a profound impact on European thought and lifestyles. The exploitative economy that the acquisition of raw materials was based on brought material well-being to Europe and facilitated an unprecedented period of growth. Colonialism is associated with an economic boom that further accelerated the rise of consumer culture in the west.

The countries most forcefully practising colonialist politics were Great Britain, France, Germany and Italy, but feelings of cultural superiority and an attitude of subjection were to be found everywhere in Europe. On a global scale, there existed a division of labour of sorts among the major European powers: French interest focused on Indo-China, North Africa and Madagascar, Germany's on South-West Africa and Italy's on East Africa. The strongest colonial power was, however, Britain, whose seat of world domination was in India, especially after Queen Victoria was crowned Empress of India on 28 April 1876. Another important area for expansion was South Africa, where diamond and gold findings emphasized the economic significance of the area. The third base was Egypt, which, after the completion of the Suez Canal in 1869, became an important gate between Europe and Asia. At the turn of the century the British controlled 20 per cent of the world's surface area and 25 per cent of the population.[3]

Many Europeans perceived colonial power as a mission which took civilization beyond the oceans. In his journal entry in 1836, Charles Darwin revealingly wrote: 'It is impossible for an Englishman to behold these distant colonies without a high pride and satisfaction. To hoist the British flag seems to draw with it as a certain consequence, wealth, prosperity, and civilisation.'[4] Colonial culture, which can in many respects be characterized as a plunder economy, was seen, or at least expressed, in terms of the cultivation of wealth, progress and civilization that would come to benefit the target area. When Jules Verne published his adventure novel *Five Weeks in a Balloon* in 1863, the colonial race into Africa had already started. Together with his friend Dick Kennedy, Verne's Doctor Ferguson travels over Africa in a balloon named after Queen Victoria. During the flight the travellers discuss European expansion, but Ferguson interprets it in an ambivalent way. The natural resources of North America were already under frantic exploitation, and Africa was the next target. Ferguson reflects:

> Thus, we already see the millions rushing to the luxuriant bosom of America, as a source of help, not inexhaustible indeed, but not yet exhausted. In its turn, that new continent will grow old; its virgin forests will fall before the axe of industry, and its soil will become weak through having too fully produced what had been demanded of it. Where two harvests bloomed every year, hardly one will be gathered from a soil completely drained of its strength. Then, Africa will be there to offer to new races the treasures that for centuries have been accumulating in her breast. Those climates now so fatal to strangers will be purified by cultivation and by drainage of the soil, and those scattered water supplies will be gathered into one common bed to form an artery of navigation. Then this country over which we are now passing, more fertile, richer, and fuller of vitality than the rest, will become some grand realm where more astonishing discoveries than steam and electricity will be brought to light.[5]

Although there is an obvious hint of criticism in Ferguson's reference to the destruction of the forests and the impoverishment of the African soil, the ultimate solution lies in western rationality.

'Astonishing discoveries' will be made in Africa, too, after the continent has been 'drained'. There might be a shadow of doubt to be discerned in this antagonism, but Ferguson's view is laced with deep technophilia.[6] The relationship between Europe and Africa is explicit enough, however: the continent has rich natural resources – and probably it will, in the future, also have a civilization, born under European influence. Yet it seems that, in Ferguson's view, the local culture has nothing genuine to offer.

Although contemporaries saw the relationship as one-sided, its effects travelled in both directions. As a cultural process, colonialism could be called one of transculturation: impulses moved both ways.[7] These impulses were both mental and material.[8] The role of missionary work was quite central in imperialist self-understanding, however. This view is often perceived as having been best interpreted by Rudyard Kipling (1865–1936) in his poem 'The White Man's Burden'. Born in Bombay, Kipling spent his childhood in India and returned there for seven years as a journalist in the 1880s. In 1889 he resettled in England, achieving recognition with his poems, short stories and novels dealing with India. The best known of these are the short stories collected in the two volumes of the *Jungle Book* (1894–5) and the novel *Kim* (1901).

The poem 'The White Man's Burden' can be interpreted in various ways, even though its first verse appears to be openly propagandist:

> Take up the White Man's burden –
> Send forth the best ye breed –
> Go bind your sons to exile
> To serve your captives' need;
> To wait in heavy harness
> On fluttered folk and wild –
> Your new-caught, sullen peoples,
> Half devil and half child.[9]

The view taken by the poem of residents of the colony is bleak; they are not only related to children and devils but also sullen and ungrateful. The tone of the poem is ambivalent from the very first verses as revealed by the paradoxical characterization of colonial masters as 'serving their captives' need'. The white man's burden is to sacrifice the best of its powers on the altar of spreading western civilization. Conflicting feelings are also reflected by the fact that those 'in heavy harness' are not the subjected peoples but the victors themselves, bound by obligation. The task of the white man is to control his own emotions: 'In patience to abide . . .' Feelings of fear need to be restrained, pride must be forgotten and the goal is one of purposefulness: 'By open speech and simple, an hundred times made plain . . .' Perhaps Kipling's verses seemed critical to contemporaries; the author's aim was, after all, to deprive colonial administration of its loftiness or brilliance. The white man of Kipling's poem fights illness and malnutrition: he is an unselfish benefactor, or at least should be. At the same time he is also a role model, a moral example:

> Take up the White Man's burden –
> Ye dare not stoop to less –
> Nor call too loud on Freedom
> To cloak your weariness;
> By all ye cry or whisper,
> By all ye leave or do,
> The silent, sullen peoples
> Shall weigh your Gods and you.[10]

'The White Man's Burden' explicitly addresses the meeting of cultures: economic and political exploitation is disguised as a battle against heathenness, hunger and disease, waged selflessly by the 'white man'. These were undoubtedly the arguments brought up in propaganda to justify the acts committed in the name of colonial government. In the poem, Kipling seems to be speaking directly and without hesitation, but at other times, in the *Jungle Book*, for example, his comments are usually veiled. Although the work describes the world of the boy Mowgli, Baloo the Bear and Bagheera the Panther, as well as of many other residents of the jungle, the stories reveal a faith in law and order, and in a just life. At the core of the *Jungle Book* is the law of the jungle that all occupants must follow.[11] Perhaps Kipling really believed that in the human world, too, abiding by the law would make possible the coexistence of Europe and Asia. In Kipling's world the victors have obligations towards the vanquished and governance is fundamentally unselfish.

Almost an opposite of Kipling's image can be found in *The Heart of Darkness* (1902) by the Polish-English author Joseph Conrad. The central character in the work is the ivory agent Kurtz, who, on arriving in Africa, had had high ideals, but very quickly lost all sense of proportion in an environment where the whims of the white man had no holds. In Conrad's world ideals were replaced by emptiness. 'His was an impenetrable darkness,' writes Conrad of Kurtz, 'I looked at him as you peer down at a man who is lying at the bottom of a precipice where the sun never shines.'[12]

Although Kipling's 'White Man's Burden' is often used as an example of colonialist wilfulness and racism, Kipling's worldview is intensely moral and – compared to Conrad's – optimistic. Many of his works are contradictory in that he feels strong sympathy with the conquered yet at the same time emphasizes the important role of the elite white culture. In his poem 'Gunga Din' (1892), this ambivalence is interestingly present. Written in a robust style, the poem describes the wretched fate of an Indian soldier. He is shouted at and spoken to harshly, and even called a 'squidgy-nosed old idol'. Despite this, Gunga Din carries out his tasks meticulously:

> 'E would dot an' carry one
> Till the longest day was done;
> An' 'e didn't seem to know the use o' fear.
> If we charged or broke or cut,
> You could bet your bloomin' nut,
> 'E'd be waitin' fifty paces right flank rear.
> With 'is mussick on 'is back,
> 'E would skip with our attack,
> An' watch us till the bugles made 'Retire',
> An' for all 'is dirty 'ide
> 'E was white, clear white, inside
> When 'e went to tend the wounded under fire![13]

When taking care of his tasks, the man with the 'dirty hide' was 'white' on the inside. This comment could surely not have meant that ethnic overlap had removed the idea of the inequality between the races. Kipling's world – like the colonial world in general – was based on inequality. Despite this, the author shows a willingness to understand and appreciate the other, especially since, born in India, Kipling was a citizen of two worlds. On the other hand, Gunga Din's 'whiteness' was perhaps an indication of faith in the positive outcome of the European project of enlightenment.

The idea of the inequality of races presented by the French count Joseph Arthur de Gobineau (1816–82) in his *Essai sur l'iné- galité des races humaines* (1853–5) was influential in the worldview of colonialist culture. This point of view had a significant impact on European anti-Semitism and racism, which became stronger with the passing of the century. De Gobineau's thoughts found a keen response especially in Germany, where racial doctrines received increasing support from the 1870s onward.[14] De Gobineau thought of himself as a descendant of the Vikings and constructed, in his essay, the myth of the fair-haired and blue- eyed Aryan race. Through the influence of Houston Stewart Chamberlain, the idea later became a founding doctrine of the Third Reich. De Gobineau's thoughts included the idea of bio- logical characteristics determining the basis for behaviour, social relations and cultural capabilities. Ultimately, this was not simply a question of the relation between ethnic groups or nations but also of the internal hierarchies of communities. According to de Gobineau, the lower social classes were racially inferior to the upper.[15] This point of view can surely be connected with the dual- istic view of humanity that intensified at the end of the nineteenth century, with its opposition of the barbaric half animal to the civ- ilized citizen. According to racial doctrines, these extremes were not even located on the same continuum for the simple reason that their separation was based on biological differences. It is interest- ing, then, that while colonial administrations tried to find argu- ments to defend the superiority of Europeans over the people of other continents, the means for making demarcations were also constructed within European cultures. Foreign cultures were not only an external threat: they were also an internal source of fear. As a matter of fact, the first serious pogroms in Europe took place at the very time when Christendom turned against its external enemy, the Arab world, during the Crusades. In a sense, the same thing happened in the latter half of the nineteenth century. When the major European powers took control of a great part of the world the ethnic minorities within Europe were also – somewhat paradoxically – perceived as a threat. The fearsome 'other' was not only to be found outside.[16] Ultimately, the threat lay within European identity and self-understanding, which underwent great changes at the end of the nineteenth century (more on this theme in the following chapter).

Another interesting perspective on colonial culture at the end of the nineteenth century is presented by the fact that at a time when transportation and communication technology made it possible to move outside the borders of Europe and receive information and images of events in the rest of the world much faster than before, the global supremacy of European culture only intensified. While the new technology was intentionally used to extend political and economic activities, the issue was not one of simple instrumental exploitation. More important than political power was the power of information. The telegraph, the railroad and the steamship became the first building blocks of the European information society. They turned the rest of the world into an object of knowledge and thus quickly subsumed foreign cultures to European rule. Recently (post)colonial theory has emphasized the close connection between knowledge and power. Colonization is not born from political action alone. Rather, it results from the adoption of a complex, western conceptual system as a universal standard, affecting our ways of perceiving and understanding other cultures. In this form, the impact of 'colonization' is not confined to ethnic groups and different continents. It has also influenced, for example, the dialogue and relationship between the genders and social groups.

Colonial culture was not only a world of information but also of curiosity and fantasy. Distant countries captured a significant place in the European imagination, of which the fictions of Kipling and Conrad mentioned above are only minor examples. The eastern Mediterranean was a region that particularly titillated imaginations, with its tradition of Orientalism that started in the eighteenth century being strengthened in the nineteenth.[17] Travel accounts became a popular form of literature during the nineteenth century, making armchair travel available to those who would never have the opportunity to make an excursion of their own. The golden age of travel accounts continued until the First World War.[18] During the same period, the depiction of exotic places became common in popular visual culture. Stereoscopic images and magic lantern presentations of the rainforests of Africa, the pyramids of Egypt or the miracles of the Holy Land became available to Europeans at reasonable prices. In Britain, echoes of the Empire were to be heard even in music halls. In the 1880s one of the most popular performers was Leo Dryden, who, dressed as a Maharajah, sang the song 'India's Reply'. The theme of imperialism was, in fact, strongly present in music hall entertainment, comments on topical political events were made on all fronts and the British soldier forced to venture out into the wide world was glorified.[19] In 1881 Leslie Stuart wrote for Albert Christian the song 'Soldiers of the Queen' with the aim of awakening Britain to the imminent danger:

> War clouds gather over every land
> Our treaties threaten'd East and West.
> Nations we've shaken by the hand
> Our honoured pledges try to test.[20]

At the end of the nineteenth century exceptionally pompous stage entertainment was produced, in which the theatrical spectacle was used to portray the activities of British troops on land and water and the history of imperial conquest was depicted through theatrical means. Justification was sought for in the past too, by comparing the conquests of the British Empire to the expansion of the ancient Roman Empire. At the turn of the century lavish historical spectacles with themes drawn from antiquity, such as *Quo Vadis*, *The Last Days of Pompeii* and *Ben Hur*, were popular alongside accounts of more recent imperial history. Large group scenes, battles reenacted on stage and showy pyrotechnical effects were typical of such shows. Researchers have since concluded that these spectacular dramas were of particular significance to the development of historical films later on. In any event, ancient Rome and Great Britain came together in these dramas. At the same time, the decadent life of antiquity offered an opportunity to depict abundance and sensuality within the confines of Victorian morality.[21]

An interesting aspect of colonial culture was demonstrated by the anthropological and ethnographical exhibitions organized in Europe. Especially in England, the conquest of Africa was displayed in many exhibitions in the 1890s and at the beginning of the twentieth century. At the 1890 Stanley and African exhibition in the Victoria Gallery, visitors to the gallery were interestingly placed in the boots of the explorer, and had the opportunity of tracing the footsteps of Henry Morton Stanley himself across the Congo. The entrance to the exhibition was framed by tree trunks, as if the visitor were entering a rainforest in Africa. Next, the visitor would come across an explorer's camp, surrounded by pictures and objects imitating the central African landscape. Africa was transformed into a fictive whole. After the camp, the visitor could become acquainted with portraits of the monarchs. On display were above all those British and Belgian monarchs, seen to have furthered the conquest of Africa. Beside these pictures was one of Stanley himself, portrayed as the most significant explorer of the time. The exhibition itself offered images of weapons, clothing, sculpture and crafts of the central African tribes. At the same time, features that demonstrated the humanitarian and philanthropic nature of the European mission were intentionally emphasized. The exhibition stressed the centrality of slave trade in the internal relations between tribes. The objective was to present the urgency of colonial action: the British were bringing a humane touch to darkest Africa, unlike the Germans, who were also hurrying to the area from East Africa.[22]

The Stanley and African exhibition created an imaginary expedition, enabling visitors to imagine what it was like to wander in the jungle and on the savannah. Towards the end of the nineteenth century actual travel also increased, with tourism being increasingly directed beyond the borders of Europe. Also in this respect, the British were predecessors. Thomas Cook (1808–92) had begun organizing packaged tours as early as 1841, when he had transported 570 passengers by train to a temperance meeting in Loughborough, 20 kilometres from Leicester.[23] By degrees, Cook's business expanded and packaged tours to the Mediterranean started. Increasingly, after the 1880s, the bases of the British Empire, above all Egypt, Palestine and India, became the destinations of travel. Cook's – and his son John Mason Cook's – company opened an office in Bombay as early as 1881 and in Calcutta in 1883. At the end of the 1880s the number of travellers was still small, but during the next decade record levels of growth were reached. While Cook had taken almost 1,000 people to Egypt and Palestine during 1889–90, the season from 1897–8 saw 50,000 British travelling to Egypt alone. At the same time, the pattern for modern mass tourism evolved. Interestingly, colonialism and tourism were already linked at this early stage – travel was not only about holidaying abroad. Behind it lay the conscious intention of becoming acquainted with new members of the commonwealth. The strategic sites of imperial history became popular destinations along with places of religious significance. Lucknow, Delhi and Kanpur, the sites of the battles of the Sepoy Mutiny of 1857 in India, were important destinations for pilgrimage. Travel agents to Africa naturally drew attention to the mythic heroes of the colonial wars. Journeys to the Nile in the 1890s acknowledged the martyrdom of General Gordon during the Mahdi Rebellion in Sudan in 1885, when the city of Khartoum was conquered. Colonial tourism was, above all, the pleasure of the upper and middle classes; the majority of the population had to make do with virtual journeys in the form of diorama presentations and magic lantern displays.[24]

An interesting, and so far relatively little studied, aspect of colonial culture is the reformulation of the European historical consciousness at the end of the nineteenth century and at the beginning of the twentieth. In Europe, the 'governing' of foreign countries and continents often took on a scientific guise. Cultures were displayed, collected in museums and archived. This was a part of the process of creating western scientific domination. Colonial power affected this scientific activity concretely by 'improving' the working conditions of researchers in, for example, Africa or Asia. Especially archaeological excavations could pick the fruits of military conquest: in addition to supplying raw materials, colonies became a source of history. Thus, the grip that western culture had of its colonies did not only concentrate on the here and now, but extended beyond it to the past, to treasures that could be easily moved to the collections of western museums.

Interest in archaeological activity had increased significantly since the German Heinrich Schliemann had carried out excavations in Asia Minor and discovered the legendary city of Troy between 1870 and 1873.[25] It was not long before scientific excavations were also begun in Giza in Egypt under the direction of Flinders Petrie in 1880. Egypt remained the treasure trove for British archaeologists until the 1920s. Despite protests, Howard Carter and his team began excavations in the Valley of the Kings in 1917, and found fame with the discovery of Tutankhamen's tomb in 1922.[26] In ancient Babylonia, the land of the Twin Rivers, excavations were carried out by an expedition led by archaeologist Robert Koldewey from 1899 to 1917. The First World War did not prevent the research, quite the opposite. Koldewey continued his work despite adverse conditions, and managed to take a significant part of his discoveries to Germany as spoils of war. The Pergamon Museum in Berlin is an impressive monument to German colonialism: an entire Babylonian street with its gates and tiled walls has been brought to its collections.[27]

The major European museums such as the British Museum in London or the Louvre in Paris contain a vast amount of material provided by colonialist culture. This is part of a historical heritage whose fate has still to be finally decided. To whom do these memorials belong? Who owns history? Such fruits of archaeological expeditions bear continued testimony to the impact of colonial culture. Colonialism has been an important element in the construction of European identity and, through it, power has extended its reach to influence conceptions of both knowledge and history.

9
Fin de Siècle: *The End of a Century*

With the approach of the turn of the century, Europeans began to call the period they were living in the *fin de siècle*, the end of the century. It seems that the term was in common use already during the 1880s, although it is best known from a journal founded by Édouard Dujardin bearing the same name, the first issue of which appeared in France in 1890. *Fin de siècle* commonly referred to unfavourable omens, according to which western culture was gradually declining and little could be expected from the new century in the way of positive developments.[1]

One background factor was the social break brought about by industrialization: urbanization was at its peak in the 1880s and the 1890s. The population of Berlin, for example, doubled during the last two decades of the century, finally exceeding the two-million mark. The problem of 'excess population' was most obvious as vagrancy, which was assumed in the long run to lead to immorality. Moral panic was an inevitable consequence. Understandably, it was especially the large centres that were in a crisis and, amid the surprising changes that had taken place, opinions concerning the way things would continue to develop could not be very well grounded. This added to feelings of insecurity. Towards the end of the century, the environmental effects of industrialization were plain to see and attitudes to technological development were no longer as optimistic as they had been only a few decades earlier. Demands by workers and women for their civil rights also increased at the end of the century. Both movements had been born in Europe around the time that industrialization began to establish its position in the economy. A problem in its own right was caused by the fact that while industry transformed society and culture greatly and demanded unrestricted mobility from the population, the old class society was still in place. Behind the *fin de siècle* culture lay this opposition, that was ultimately reflected as a conflict within the society's moral conceptions, values and ideologies.

These conflicts were also present in the view of human nature, which had undergone interesting changes during the century. Natural sciences, such as medicine and chemistry, placed a special emphasis on the biological understanding of life, also accentuating the impact of science on everyday life. An interest in organic chemistry had already appeared at the beginning of the nineteenth century and created the basis for modern medicine. The German physiologist Theodor Schwann (1810–82) argued in the 1830s that the cell was the basic unit for the functions of the human body. The possibilities for public health services improved when the French chemist and microbiologist Louis Pasteur (1822–95) showed the meaning of bacteria and vaccination in the treatment of diseases and developed, for example, a vaccination against rabies. The German physician Robert Koch (1843–1910), in turn, conducted groundbreaking research on infectious diseases and general bacteriology. In medicine, the increase of autopsies and the development of microscopy were essential background factors.[2] This history of scientific developments can be seen as a story of progress but, at the same time, especially towards the end of the century, it meant the growing hold of science on everyday life and an ever-increasing manipulation, even medicalization, of the human body. The first operation using ether anaesthesia took place in 1846 – and this miracle of being able to manipulate the body was publicized through photography, although the daguerreotype in question was a simulation, a scene staged only for the camera.

In 1895, Louis Pasteur died in St Cloud outside Paris. His funeral was arranged in a spectacular manner, showing that he really was regarded as an embodiment of the century of science.[3] Another eminent figure to become an epitome of the mastery of science over nature was the English naturalist Charles Darwin (1809–82). In his *On the Origin of Species* (1859), he applied to nature the idea of the struggle for survival. Darwin had been influenced by the economist Thomas Malthus and his theory that the population grew faster than the supply of food. In this process the weak were inevitably eliminated along the way. Darwin's theory proved to be a scientific success, and the work quickly found its way to international forums as well. It was translated into German and Dutch in 1860 and into French a year later.[4] Darwin's theory of evolution is summarized by the last sentences of *On the Origin of Species* in which he paints an almost cosmic picture of the gradual complexification of life on earth through evolution:

> Thus, from the war of nature, from famine and death, the most exalted object which we are capable of conceiving, namely, the production of the higher animals, directly follows. There is grandeur in this view of life, with its several powers, having been originally breathed by the Creator into a few forms or into one; and that, whilst this planet has gone cycling on according to the fixed law of gravity, from so simple a beginning endless forms most beautiful and most wonderful have been, and are being, evolved.[5]

Darwin did not tackle the evolution of humanity until his *Descent of Man*, published in 1871, provoking strong criticism. The very thought that human beings had not been created as they were but had gradually evolved to their present state was enough to shock traditional values, especially those of the gentility. It inevitably provoked a question: if mankind had an ancestry spanning countless generations, could something of this barbaric heritage still exist in spite of all attempts at civilization? And, further, if 'the Creator' had 'breathed' the life into a chosen few or only into one life-form, did not all of humanity share a common history? We can imagine the confusion that this thought created in Europeans in the heyday of colonial culture. Darwin's thesis seemed to prove that the inhabitants of all continents shared the same biological ancestry and were thus distantly related.

It may seem paradoxical that while this shared origin could have provided an opportunity for a new kind of ethnic understanding, these fresh insights into humankind's past were also accepted as grounds for inequality. Social-Darwinism, defended by Herbert Spencer (1820–1903), was an ideology that had taken its inspiration from Darwinism and that provided prosperous members of industrial society with a means of accommodating their evolutionary views to their privilege and wealth at the expense of the masses. According to the social-Darwinist point of view, social life also involved a process of selection that led to inequality. Thus the imbalance was natural.[6]

Darwin's views offered a point of contact for diverse social ideologies, even racist arguments for inequality. At the end of *On the Origin of Species*, Darwin writes of the 'higher animals' in reference to the way in which nature continually creates more beautiful forms through evolution. He most certainly was not referring to the kind of superiority presented by Count de Gobineau in his 1853–5 work on the inequality of human races, yet these viewpoints could be combined: if the evolution of more primitive and more superior species was to be found in the biological past, why could these evolutionary differences not also coexist, some races being more evolved than others? It was precisely on this idea that the racial doctrines receiving increased support in Europe in the 1870s and the subsequent decades were based. The rise of these doctrines was especially strong in Germany in the decades after the *Reichsgründung*, the German unification, and their popularity continued, in practice, until the Second World War – with devastating consequences.

Although racial doctrines had more to do with conceptions of non-European cultures, they also played a part in activating anti-Semitism, anti-Jewish sentiments and action. In Germany the concept of 'anti-Semitism' is thought to have first appeared in 1879 in Wilhelm Marr's text *Das Sieg des Judentums über das Germanentum*. By the following year Adolf Stöcker had established an anti-Semitic party called the Berliner Bewegung, which quite knowingly pursued anti-Semitic politics.[7] The new anti-Semitism differed greatly from earlier anti-Jewish sentiments. It had its basis in a view of racial character as fundamentally biological as defined by the racial doctrines. Jewishness was no longer defined as a nationality that could be integrated into the larger community or as a religion that one could convert from but as an essentialist biological phenomenon one could not escape from. The anti-Semitic movement began to pursue openly discriminatory politics, which completely excluded Jews from the community. Considering the situation in Germany, it should be added that the rise of anti-Semitism can, in part, be explained by the social changes that had taken place following the unification of Germany in 1871. The Constitution of the new Germany was in fact one of the most democratic in Europe. It gave equal civic rights to all, including the Jews. In consequence, many Jews moved from eastern European ghettos to Germany, where their civic rights were noticeably better. At the same time, the economic situation was rapidly deteriorating, giving rise to hostility towards the immigrants. This environment generated an atmosphere of intolerance whose effects were felt well into the twentieth century.[8]

The strengthening of racial doctrines was part of the triumphal march of the end-of-the-century biological view of human nature. These changes cannot, of course, be blamed on Charles Darwin – at stake was a much more general phenomenon related to people's changing life circumstances. However, Darwin's ideas can be connected to another dimension, which was the increasingly dualistic view of human nature. If humanity had a more primitive ancestry, a barbaric identity might still exist. Evolutionary biology did not in itself lead to ideas of cultural change, but culture and biology were often presented as interconnected. Primitiveness appeared as deformity, crouching posture, hairiness, and sexuality.

The Scottish author Robert Louis Stevenson put into words the conception of a dualistic human nature in his classic horror story *The Strange Case of Dr Jekyll and Mr Hyde* (1886). The novel tells the story of Doctor Henry Jekyll, who, through a potion he has concocted, turns into the evil Edward Hyde. At the end of the book Jekyll gives an account of his experiences. At the same time he describes the transformation from a civilized citizen to a cruel barbarian:

> The most racking pangs succeeded: a grinding in the bones, deadly nausea, and a horror of the spirit that cannot be exceeded at the hour

of birth or death. Then these agonies began swiftly to subside, and I came to myself as if out of a great sickness. There was something strange in my sensations, something indescribably new and, from its very novelty, incredibly sweet. I felt younger, lighter, happier in body; within I was conscious of a heady recklessness, a current of disordered sensual images running like a millrace in my fancy, a solution of the bonds of obligation, an unknown but not an innocent freedom of the soul. I knew myself, at the first breath of this new life, to be more wicked, tenfold more wicked, sold a slave to my original evil; and the thought, in that moment, braced and delighted me like wine. I stretched out my hands, exulting in the freshness of these sensations; and in the act, I was suddenly aware that I had lost in stature.[9]

At the moment of metamorphosis, Jekyll's bones tighten and he feels excruciating pain for the simple reason that the change affects his body as well as his soul. In a way, Jekyll is reborn, and thus feels himself to be younger. Having become Hyde, he is no longer bound by the obligations of civilization. He feels that his imagination and his senses have been set free. The intellect has been supplanted by emotions and 'sensual images'. He no longer possesses the critical powers and consideration instilled by civilization – and thus he delights in his evil as if it were wine. In Stevenson's interpretation evil, emotions, sensual pleasure and physicality are all intertwined. Outward appearance is defined by character, by one's inner world. This conception is not solely the product of the author's imagination since, at the time, anthropologists were trying to identify physical regularities not only in different races but also among members of different social classes. A scientific movement called phrenology collected human types both through means of photographs and numerical data. There existed a firm conviction that the physical properties of criminals, for example, showed uniformities.[10] This conviction may also be seen in Stevenson's novel:

The evil side of my nature, to which I had now transferred the stamping efficacy, was less robust and less developed than the good which I had just deposed. Again, in the course of my life, which had been, after all, nine tenths a life of effort, virtue and control, it had been much less exercised and much less exhausted. And hence, as I think, it came about that Edward Hyde was so much smaller, slighter and younger than Henry Jekyll. Even as good shone upon the countenance of the one, evil was written broadly and plainly on the face of the other. Evil besides (which I must still believe to be the lethal side of man) had left on that body an imprint of deformity and decay. And yet when I looked upon that ugly idol in the glass, I was conscious of no repugnance, rather of a leap of welcome. This, too, was myself. It seemed natural and human.[11]

According to Stevenson, evil left the body 'deformed and decayed'. Evil also consumed people, and therefore criminals were shorter. The final distinguishing feature was the face, and kindness was certainly absent from Hyde's physiognomy: evil was 'written broadly and plainly' across his countenance. In *Dr Jekyll and Mr Hyde*, good and evil inhabit the same person. As Stevenson states, 'all human beings . . . are commingled out of good and evil'. Even then, it seems that Jekyll and Hyde are also two different people, two distinct individuals. Stevenson describes the metamorphosis as a moment of life and death: as Jekyll dies, Hyde is born. This interpretation is confirmed by the social context in which the novel was written. In the London of the late 1880s, the poor of the suburban districts were seen as distinctly separate from the gentility. From this viewpoint, Stevenson's novel can be seen as depicting the duality perceived in human nature at the time, and the story of Jekyll and Hyde need not be read as a story of the fate of a single individual. In contextualizing Stevenson's novel, an interesting addition is brought by the juiciest crime story of the time. Contemporaries saw a parallel between Stevenson's story, especially its theatrical rendition, and Jack the Ripper, who terrorized London's East End. Indeed, the idea came about that Jack was a local doctor, who spent his spare time wandering the poorer districts murdering prostitutes. Here, then, the duality attributed to human nature had reached absurd proportions. A person could turn around to reveal a completely different character, and a fearsomely alien one at that.[12]

As the turn of the century approached, the concept of human nature changed in other ways, partly due to the increase in psychological studies during the latter half of the nineteenth century.

Special attention was paid to traumatic neuroses, which were found, for example, in mental problems that followed accidents. Neuroses also interested the Austrian doctor and psychiatrist Sigmund Freud (1856–1939), who gradually arrived at wholly new views on sexuality. Freud observed that mental functions are largely subconscious and that a person's drives begin to develop in early childhood and not during puberty as had previously been assumed. Freud also developed the method of psychoanalysis for the treatment of mental disorders.

Freud had studied medicine in the 1870s when Darwin and other scholars were already developing the new biological worldview. In 1885 he received a grant that enabled him to study in Paris under the neurologist Jean Martin Charcot (1825–93). Charcot utilized hypnosis in his attempts to find a physiological explanation for hysteria. On returning to Vienna, Freud began his own experiments with hypnosis. At the same time he started work on a form of treatment in which patients could themselves discover, and become conscious of, the reasons for their symptoms. This led to the method of 'free association' in the 1890s.[13] At the very end of the century, Freud published his book *The Interpretation of Dreams* (*Die Traumdeutung*, 1899). In addition to the wish-fulfilling nature of dreams the work introduced the idea of the Oedipus complex, the significance of early childhood in the development of personality, and the role of dreams in reflecting the subconscious psyche.[14]

More astounding to contemporaries were, however, his *Three Essays on the Theory of Sexuality* (*Drei Abhandlungen zur Sexualtheorie*) which appeared in 1905, their central argument being that strong evidence of sexuality was already apparent in children.[15] Freud received fierce opposition from the scientific world, but in the long run he significantly influenced views on sexuality, especially by questioning the concept of normality. Human sexuality came to be seen as a broader and more complex question than before. Another question is the extent to which this understanding spread and was accepted. Freud's views spread during several decades, but new interpretations based on them arose relatively quickly. By 1908, Freud was surrounded by a group interested in psychoanalysis, including Alfred Adler (1870–1937) and Carl Gustav Jung (1875–1961) who later broke away from the group.[16]

Sigmund Freud's work was part of the break in conceptions of human nature at the turn of the century. With his case studies he also painted a portrait of the Viennese gentility and its mental landscape at the *fin de siècle*. Freud's accounts provide a unique view of the narrow lives of the bourgeoisie at the end of the nineteenth and beginning of the twentieth centuries in which neuroses were a part of everyday life.[17] One of Freud's most interesting cases was known as the case of 'Dora'. Dora, whose real name was Ida Bauer, was the daughter of a wealthy Jewish family, her father a well-known industrialist and his younger brother Otto a leading figure in the Austrian Social Democratic Party in the years between the wars. Ida was sent to Freud by her father, who had earlier been to see him for the treatment of a sexually transmitted disease. Ida had begun acting erratically in the family circle and had even threatened suicide. In this situation, the eighteen-year-old Ida could have had no idea of the doctor's methods, but told her story anyway. Dora's case revealed a stifling and depressing family situation: the mother suffered from 'housewife psychosis', the father was having an affair with the wife of a family friend, who had, in turn, been harassing Ida for a number of years. The tragic nature of the account is reinforced by the fact that Freud did not seem to understand the social realities hidden behind the situation. Indeed, the psychoanalyst attempted to show that Ida's suffering resulted from her inability to come to terms with her own sexuality. Research has, however, ascertained that Ida was in fact a victim of a barter, the father having offered his daughter in exchange to the husband of his mistress, allowing it all to happen. According to the case report, Freud seems to have understood this 'conspiracy' and to have believed Ida's story, yet given no weight to the situation in explaining his patient's hysterical behaviour, preferring, rather, to emphasize Ida's childhood experiences and the significance of suppressed sexuality. Dora's case was not just a bitter account of the life of Viennese gentry but also demonstrated the limitations of Freud's methods.[18]

Many of Sigmund Freud's patients suffered from neuroses and hysteria. At the end of the nineteenth century Freud's theories were still relatively unknown, and there were a number of competing theories of the origins of mental disorders. Many authors, even doctors and psychiatrists, saw hysteria as a female problem. The gendered understanding of hysterical symptoms had deep roots in nineteenth-century medicine, and this tradition is still visible in Freud's analyses. Often hysteria was associated with the decadence of the time, and it was seen as part of the gradual triumph of European degeneration. Freud departed, however, in many other ways from the standard ideas of his age – his views on sexuality were radically new. In the long run, this has had a significant impact on interpretations of normality as well as of sexual deviance. Despite this, many contemporaries clung to the narrow-minded views of sexuality. Homosexuality, for instance, received little acceptance or understanding, as clearly evidenced by Oscar Wilde's trial in 1895. As a matter of fact, public opinion associated homosexuality, like hysteria, with the decadence of the age.[19]

Discussions of European *fin de siècle* art frequently refer to decadent literature and visual arts as styles in their own right. The word 'decadence' originated in a sonnet by Paul Verlaine, and in literature came to signify a counter-tendency to realist and naturalist narration. Decadent art was characterized by an intentionally bohemian attitude, the pain and suffering of life as an artist. Tragic sensual enjoyment and openly passive resignation to the social changes of the time appeared as a counterweight to this mental anguish. In a sense, decadent literature reversed nineteenth-century values: portrayals focused on decay instead of progress, losers instead of victors, illness instead of health, death instead of life . . . Favoured themes were fatal women, androgynes, incestuous love, degenerate geniuses, morbid sensitivity and broken families. Illness became a cultural metaphor of the last decades of the century: the whole era was often associated with the sick body that was gradually fading away. The metaphor is not surprising in the sense that Romantic thought had been fascinated by death throughout the century. Mortal thoughts, withering diseases and images of death were often depicted and dealt with both in literature and art.

This nihilistic attitude to life was inspired, above all, by three thinkers: Arthur Schopenhauer (1788–1860), Richard Wagner (1813–83) and Friedrich Nietzsche (1844–1900).[20] Particularly Nietzsche's thoughts appealed to the turn-of-the-century youth. The philosophy of Nietzsche – like that of Schopenhauer – excited debate concerning European values as well as the role of religion and the meaning of life. In his magnum opus *The World as Will and Representation* (*Die Welt als Wille und Vorstellung*, 1818), Schopenhauer had already presented the essence of human beings as a natural drive, an irrational life force. Life appeared as a meaningless, insatiable endeavour, and only artistic contemplation offered momentary respite from its frantic tumult. These thoughts were a source of inspiration not only to Nietzsche, but above all to Wagner, who, in his *Tristan and Isolde*, offered a musical counterpart to Schopenhauer's introspective world. Especially French authors made frequent reference to Wagner's work. Joris K. Huysmans (1848–1907) composed a paraphrase of Wagner's *Tannhäuser* overture. Huysmans's best-known work is, however, the novel *À rebours* (1884), which portrays an aesthete accumulating sensual pleasures and inhabiting a hermetic world, sophisticated yet pronouncedly artificial. Another adaptation of this Wagnerian theme was the Italian author Gabriele d'Annunzio's *Triumph of Death* (*Il trionfo della morte*, 1894), which faithfully follows in the footsteps of Wagner and Nietzsche.[21]

Whereas the public largely associated these portrayals of decadence with the feelings of ending experienced as the turn of the century approached, the artists themselves perceived their work more as a criticism of earlier art than an omen of things to come. Since the visual arts moved increasingly further from realism at the end of the century, this atmosphere of change was experienced in artistic circles more widely. When mass production of photographs began and mimetic likeness was within everyone's reach, painters increasingly gave up the pursuit of an appearance of reality. Impressionists such as Édouard Manet, Claude Monet and August Renoir had been influential since the 1860s and the 1870s; the Modernist movement continued until the First World War. On the eve of the war, the European art world was being dramatically shaped by expressionism, cubism, surrealism and futurism.

The Modernist breakthrough in the visual arts as well as in literature and music was, no doubt, bound to cause anxiety. Art was, however, the concern of only a few, most particularly of the middle class, who had been the main force in the shaping of the nineteenth-century art scene. The views associated with the consequences of technological development at the end of the century were of an even more pessimistic nature. As already noted in the first chapter, it was at the end of the nineteenth century that industrial society began to arrive at a crisis. There was an increased awareness of the destruction of the environment, the first nature reserves were founded, forest protection received extensive social support and even more attention was given to the disposal of sewage. At the same time, views of technology changed. Technical tools were no longer presented simply as providers of material prosperity, improving production, but also as containing the potential for destruction, as something that could throw European culture off course. Accidents caused by industry or transportation increased, further highlighting the possibility of catastrophe.

The changed attitude towards technology can be especially well seen in the work of one author, the French writer Jules Verne (1828–1905). Verne took a close interest in topical debates and collected newspaper and journal clippings. His use of this material is notable in his series *Extraordinary Voyages* (*Voyages extraordinaires*, 1862–1919), which included sixty-five novels and eighteen stories, the first novel being *Five Weeks in a Balloon* (*Cinq semaines en ballon*), published in Paris in 1863.[22] In this novel, as in all of his work, Verne's view of science and its possibilities is optimistic. Yet *Five Weeks in a Balloon* also contains a gloomy prophecy. The hunter Dick Kennedy speculates on the possibility of a colossal steam-engine:

> By dint of inventing machinery, men will end in being eaten up by it! I have always fancied that the end of the earth will be when some enormous boiler, heated to three thousand millions of atmospheric pressure, shall explode and blow up our Globe![23]

Kennedy's nightmarish vision represents a critique of technology that is fairly uncommon in Verne's early work, although the opinion is attributed here to the fictional character. Works such as *Journey to the Centre of the Earth* (*Voyage au centre de la terre*, 1864), *From the Earth to the Moon* (*De la terre à la lune*, 1865), *Round the Moon* (*Autour de la lune*, 1870), *Twenty Thousand Leagues under the Seas* (*Vingt mille lieues sous les mers*, 1870) and *Around the World in Eighty Days* (*Le Tour du monde en quatre-vingts jours*, 1873), for example, are more representative of the classic Verne, outlining the effects of topical, well-known or probable scientific achievements. As a matter of fact, the central aim of many of the novels was either to verify or disprove some scientific theory or claim. This story-type is even represented by a title such as *Robur the Conqueror* (*Robert-le-conquérant*) which appeared as late as 1886, and focused on a single, specific problem: is the future one of heavier-than-air or lighter-than-air aircraft? Typically to Verne, the story itself is not set in the future, but rather describes a situation in which present-day scientists already live in tomorrow's world, outlining solutions that are to have an effect on everyday life only after decades or even centuries. *Robur the Conqueror* ends with the heavier-than-air flying vessel *The Albatross* and its crew being forced to stay away from publicity because the time is not yet ripe for them:

> Then Robur continued.
>
> 'Citizens of the United States, my experiment is finished; but my advice to those present is to be premature in nothing, not even in progress. It is evolution and not revolution that we should seek. In a word, we must not be before our time. I have come too soon today to withstand such contradictory and divided interests as yours. Nations are not yet fit for union.'
>
> 'I go, then; and I take my secret with me. But it will not be lost to humanity. It will belong to you the day you are educated enough to profit by it and wise enough not to abuse it. Citizens of the United States – Good-by!'[24]

In Verne's early novels travel, being on the move, is an important motif. It might well represent the entire century, an era of transportation and motion, in which belief in progress remained strong until its very last decades. Verne often portrayed machines as liberators of humanity. Behind them there was always a single person, the inventor, who lived in the depths of the earth or the thickets of the jungle, in the deep of the oceans or on the unoccupied surface of the moon. Paradoxically enough, Verne's heroes often attempted to escape technological culture in order to enjoy nature. It was not customary, during the nineteenth century and even at the beginning of the twentieth century, to perceive technology as an obstacle to the symbiosis of humans and nature. The very first cars were marketed as a means for urban families to speed off to the peace and quiet of the countryside.[25] At the end of *Robur the Conqueror*, Robur, in Vernean fashion, departs from human society: he represents the future world, awaiting somewhere in the unknown:

> And now, who is this Robur? Shall we ever know?
> We know today. Robur is the science of the future. Perhaps the science of tomorrow. Certainly the science that will come![26]

In the very year that *Robur the Conqueror* was published, there was a significant turn in Verne's career. Pessimism had begun to creep into his thinking as early as 1870–1 with the Franco–Prussian War, only to be intensified by the civil war that raged in Paris in the spring of 1871. The significant turning point was, however, his becoming the target of an attempted assassination in 1886. Verne's nephew Gaston seriously wounded the author, who, in a fit of melancholy, burnt all his personal papers. In his works of the late nineteenth and early twentieth centuries scientists no longer appear as selfless representatives of the future as did Robur. In the novel *For the Flag* (*Face au drapeau*, 1896), the scientist Thomas Roch comes up with an ingenious missile that he tries to sell to the French government. He is, however, captured by the pirate Ker Karraje and is forced to develop this extremely destructive weapon for the criminals.

In Verne's later work, technology is always in danger of breaking loose from societal control. The novel *The Master of the World* (*Maître du monde*, 1904) depicts a scientist who uses modern technology for evil ends. He builds a car that travels so fast the police can do nothing. At the time of writing this novelette in 1901–2, Jules Verne was already a cynical old man, disillusioned with technology. The very title of the novel was ironic. Technology was leading to an oligarchy, the aims of which seemed unknown to everyone. Perhaps the primitive reaction towards technology demonstrated by the masses was not, after all, unfounded:

> The public imagination, highly excited, readily accepted every sort of rumor about this mysterious automobile. It was said to be a supernatural

car. It was driven by a specter, by one of the chauffeurs of hell, a goblin from another world, a monster escaped from some mythological menagerie, in short, the devil in person, who could defy all human intervention, having at his command invisible and infinite satanic powers.[27]

At the end of the nineteenth century an interest in supernatural phenomena developed alongside the questioning of the scientific-technological worldview. Among the vogues of the time was occultism, which can be interpreted as a countermove to the long reign of rationalism. Naturally, the history of occultism, secret doctrines, can be traced far into the distant past, but with the approaching end of the century the spirit world and the unknown forces within the universe fascinated Europeans. Occultism is generally taken to include spiritism, belief in demons and witches, alchemy, exorcism and magic, and the spiritist movement gained extensive support in the *fin de siècle* atmosphere. It also had a close link to the theosophical movement founded by Helena Petrovna Blavatsky (1831–91).[28] The turn-of-the-century rationalism is often exemplified by Sir Arthur Conan Doyle's (1859–1930) fictional character, detective Sherlock Holmes, who was of the opinion that even apparently supernatural phenomena always had a logical explanation. Surprisingly, however, the author himself was quite interested in the occult. Only in one of the Holmesian stories does he seem to waver between logic and the supernatural. This is the legendary detective story *The Hound of the Baskervilles* (1902). In the vicinity of the remote Baskerville estate there appears to be a supernatural – and super-historical – dog that terrorizes the area, and to which many members of the family are said to have fallen victim. The journey from London to the distant moors is like a plunge far back into history and at the same time far away from the scientific-technological culture of western civilization. In a letter to Sherlock Holmes, Doctor Watson describes this experience:

When you are once out upon its bosom you have left all traces of modern England behind you, but, on the other hand, you are conscious everywhere of the homes and the work of the prehistoric people. On all sides of you as you walk are the houses of these forgotten folk, with their graves and the huge monoliths which are supposed to have marked their temples. As you look at their gray stone huts against the scarred hillsides you leave your own age behind you, and if you were to see a skin-clad, hairy man crawl out from the low door fitting a flint-tipped arrow on to the string of his bow, you would feel that his presence there was more natural than your own.[29]

In the end, all is logically explained, in keeping with the spirit of western rationalism, but at the same time, Sir Arthur Conan Doyle reveals something of himself also, of his interest in the spirit world and in powers that are beyond the reach of logic.

Although criticism of and alternatives to the scientific-technological world existed, they had little impact on the course of rationalism. It was really the First World War that threw a dark and indelible shadow over the optimism. In the war, technology stood – and was set in – clear opposition to humans. The eruption of the war was also preceded by the century's greatest catastrophe, the sinking of the passenger ship *Titanic* on its way from Southampton to New York in the night between 14 and 15 April 1912. The ship sank amazingly fast, in three hours, and there was insufficient room in the lifeboats for all of the passengers. Immediately following the accident, the Finnish newspaper *Helsingin Sanomat* wrote:

Minds are numbed in every country on both sides of the Atlantic by the frightful ocean tragedy that swallowed half a thousand people into the night-time waves. Members of every northern and central European nation – all traversing the ocean on the Titanic – sank into their shared grave and now those nations share a common grief.[30]

This sorrow swept across Europe on the eve of the First World War. The cause of the sinking had clearly been an unfounded belief in technological progress: the captain was unable to control the ship that was designed to be larger and faster than any previous vessel. Technology simply broke loose.

10

Conclusion: 'Things to Come'

When preparations were being made for the New Year's celebrations of 31 December 1899, many contemporaries felt that a new era was beginning. As noted in the introduction, such expectations do not necessarily signify a clean break, the turning of an end into a beginning, and many features of European culture continued until the First World War. Yet the experience of contemporaries is significant. Expectations and fears associated with the future influenced the way people behaved as well as the way they reacted to events around them, and the role of the future was particularly pronounced in European thought at the end of the nineteenth century. This can be seen, for instance, in the rapid growth of utopian thought and literature.

While the utopias of early modern times were often ones of place, located on far-off islands or in distant lands, modern utopias projected their imaginary societies in time, into the distant future. The first temporal utopia is generally taken to be the French author Louis Sébastian Mercier's *L'An 2440* from the year 1770. It was not until the nineteenth century, however, that there was a real increase in the number of temporal utopias.[1] This trend can be said to encompass Karl Marx's prophecies of the future development of western society just as much as Richard Wagner's theories of the work of art in the future. The new emphasis on the future is equally demonstrated by the boom in science-fiction at the end of the century. Fantasies about the future were in demand. Bearing in mind the major socio-cultural changes taking place in Europe at the time and the increasing mobility of products and information, we can well assume that contemporaries felt the pace of change to be problematic: with such rapid changes, what could be deduced from past experiences any longer? If traditions were discontinued, what could be expected of the future? Although futurology is properly a product of the twentieth century,[2] already in the previous century, especially towards its end, there was a need to ponder the direction that changes in society and culture were taking.

Even in the field of art, future developments caused concern. The first Modernist in the history of European music was Richard Wagner who made use of such strong chromaticism in his compositions, especially in *Tristan and Isolde* and *Parsifal*, that orthodox harmonies were stretched to their limits. In theory, this prepared the way for atonal music. When Wagner published his vision of the future of artworks at the turn of the 1840s and the 1850s, conservative music circles were disconcerted by the idea that the composer's own art would provide a norm for the future.[3] It is not surprising, then, that Wagner's name appeared on the pages of utopian novels. Jules Verne mentions Wagner's ear-splitting melodies in a fantasy located in the Paris of the 1960s.[4] Also interesting is Swedish journalist Claës Lundin's novel, *Oxygen och Aromasia* (1878), which depicts Stockholm in the year 2378, governed by extreme capitalism. In Lundin's world Richard Wagner's clamorous music had caused humankind to become deaf – and thus art had taken to deploying the sense of scent:

> The Music of the Future, which had first made its breakthrough early in the nineteenth century, underwent during the succeeding two centuries such development, and achieved such a perfection, not least due to the phonograph, that it became more than the ear could bear. The famous Richard Wagner, inventor of the Music of the Future, had dealt the human eardrum such a treatment that in the end people could no longer hear anything at all; and by means of the phonograph, his disciples had sent their trombone blasts around the entire World. Mankind

had long been deaf; stone deaf; until in the end the ear became regarded as a redundant appendage to the body.

It was at this time that friends of the arts and chemists began to devote their attention to the long-disregarded nose. In the preceding centuries the sensitivity of the olfactory organ had not improved; on the contrary, it had deteriorated, on account of nicotine. Yet could not this state of affairs be amended? There is none of the human senses which affects the feelings so powerfully as that of scent. It was therefore obvious that the means of art should be deployed to make use of this sense. Thorough investigations were initiated into the distinctive character and effects of scent; the laws of olfactory harmony and disharmony were formulated, first empirically, but then in theoretical terms. Chemistry was able to supply, at steadily falling cost, the necessary scents, and once the Ododion had been publicly displayed as an astounding piece of equipment, it soon began to be deployed by artists and so, in the course of time, within the home as well. This was the end of music, and the Music of the Future had a future no more.[5]

Lundin presents Wagner's music not only as unhealthy but also as damaging. The writer is apparently informed of the phonograph patented by Edison in 1877 since he sees the new technology as posing a threat to all humanity. For it was the phonograph that enabled Wagner's melodies to circle the world. Although Lundin's work – like so many other utopian novels – is a distanciated, ironic description of the writer's own time, it also builds on developmental trends that worried his contemporaries. In particular, the increasing importance of money has transformed the Sweden of the twenty-first century into a very different kind of environment.

It would hardly be possible to discuss the fictional futures of the end of the nineteenth century without mentioning the British author H. G. Wells, whose influence, unlike that of Lundin, spanned all of Europe.[6] In his novel *The Time Machine* (1895), Wells speculates on the possibility of travelling through time and – with the help of technology – visiting the world of the future to see how things were going to change. Departing from the typical stories situated in the future, Wells's novel consists of a constant dialogue with the present – for the simple reason that the work describes time travel, thus involving passage between temporal levels. In the

novel, the protagonist arrives in the year 802,701, to a world ruled
by two races of humans, the Eloi, living on the upper world, and
the Morlocks who rule under the ground. In coming across this
division of humanity, Wells's alter ego is forced to come up with
an explanation:

> At first, proceeding from the problems of our own age, it seemed clear
> as daylight to me that the gradual widening of the present merely tem-
> porary and social difference between the Capitalist and the Labourer,
> was the key to the whole position. No doubt it will seem grotesque
> enough to you – and wildly incredible! – and yet even now there are
> existing circumstances to point that way. There is a tendency to utilize
> underground space for the less ornamental purposes of civilization;
> there is the Metropolitan Railway in London, for instance, there are
> new electric railways, there are subways, there are underground work-
> rooms and restaurants, and they increase and multiply. Evidently, I
> thought, this tendency had increased till Industry had gradually lost its
> birthright in the sky. I mean that it had gone deeper and deeper
> into larger and ever larger underground factories, spending a still-
> increasing amount of its time therein, till, in the end – ! Even now,
> does not an East-end worker live in such artificial conditions as prac-
> tically to be cut off from the natural surface of the earth?[7]

As the excerpt reveals, the starting point of Wells's novel is the class-
divided society of Britain – and perhaps of all Europe – at the end
of the nineteenth century. The connection is understandable, and
is associated with the racial doctrine claiming that evolution may
lead in two opposite directions. In Wells's view humanity had thus
arrived at a crossroads in 1895 or at least omens of future development were already to be seen, if only they could be understood.
The social gap inevitably led to a biological one:

> Again, the exclusive tendency of richer people – due, no doubt, to the
> increasing refinement of their education, and the widening gulf
> between them and the rude violence of the poor – is already leading to
> the closing, in their interest, of considerable portions of the surface of
> the land. About London, for instance, perhaps half the prettier country
> is shut in against intrusion. And this same widening gulf – which is due

to the length and expense of the higher educational process and the increased facilities for and temptations towards refined habits on the part of the rich – will make that exchange between class and class, that promotion by intermarriage which at present retards the splitting of our species along lines of social stratification, less and less frequent. So, in the end, above ground you must have the Haves, pursuing pleasure and comfort and beauty, and below ground the Have-nots, the Workers getting continually adapted to the conditions of their labour. Once they were there, they would no doubt have to pay rent, and not a little of it, for the ventilation of their caverns; and if they refused, they would starve or be suffocated for arrears. Such of them as were so constituted as to be miserable and rebellious would die; and, in the end, the balance being permanent, the survivors would become as well adapted to the conditions of underground life, and as happy in their way, as the Upper-world people were to theirs. As it seemed to me, the refined beauty and the etiolated pallor followed naturally enough.[8]

The division of humanity that had come about as a result of industrialization during the nineteenth century was, in Wells's vision, fatal and final. In addition to marking a cultural differentiation it also heralded a biological separation. The material prosperity brought about by industrialization was shrouded in pessimism. General welfare had degenerated into an idle leisured class of the wealthy in constant search of new pleasures, subjecting the workers to a bleak netherworld existence:

The great triumph of Humanity I had dreamed of took a different shape in my mind. It had been no such triumph of moral education and general co-operation as I had imagined. Instead, I saw a real aristocracy, armed with a perfected science and working to a logical conclusion the industrial system of today. Its triumph had not been simply a triumph over Nature, but a triumph over Nature and the fellow-man. This, I must warn you, was my theory at the time. I had no convenient cicerone in the pattern of the Utopian books. My explanation may be absolutely wrong. I still think it is the most plausible one. But even on this supposition the balanced civilization that was at last attained must have long since passed its zenith, and was now far fallen into decay. The too-perfect security of the Upper-worlders had led them to a slow movement of degeneration, to a general dwindling in size, strength, and intelligence. That I could see clearly enough already. What had happened to the Under-grounders I did not yet suspect; but from what I had seen of the Morlocks – that, by the by, was the name by which these creatures were called – I could imagine that the modification of the human type was even far more profound than among the 'Eloi', the beautiful race that I already knew.[9]

Wells does not even try to present his vision as a utopia, but he sees it as a credible path for development from the condition that Europe was in in the 1890s. As well as taming nature, industry had tamed humankind. In the end, the 'aristocracy' would degenerate as a result of a life of ease and comfort. In this, Wells seems to have accepted the view of human development offered by racial doctrines: the 'size, strength and intelligence' of the upper worlders had begun to 'dwindle'. The mental and physical person had become one.

While *The Time Machine* remained H. G. Wells's classic work, he wrote a number of other science-fiction novels at the turn of the century. These included *The Invisible Man* (1897), *The War of the Worlds* (1898), *When the Sleeper Wakes* (1899) and *The First Men in the Moon* (1901). Wells continued to write regularly through the years of the First World War, publishing the novel *The Shape of Things to Come* in 1933, in which the war has become a significant shaper of his visions of the future.

Before the First World War, visions of the future did not commonly foresee the possibility of a sudden catastrophe or military crisis. One of the most interesting utopian novels of the end of the nineteenth century was the American author Edward Bellamy's *Looking Backward, 2000–1887*, which gained much worldwide recognition after its publication in 1888 and was translated into more than twenty languages.[10] The story begins with Julian West, a gentleman from Boston, awakening after a 113-year-long hypnotically induced trance in the year 2000. In the world of the year 2000, no problems remain. The working day is proportionate, depending on how interested the worker is in the assigned tasks as well as on the nature of the work. Technological advances have also solved all environmental problems. Factories no longer have chimneys. Neither is there retail business in the year 2000, since citizens purchase all their goods with credit cards from large, centralized stores. By the turn of the millennium, equality between men and women has also been realized.

Bellamy's socialist utopia is in complete opposition to the world of Wells's *Time Machine* – at least to the extent that, in a way, *Looking Backward* shows a future in which humanity has succeeded in solving its problems. On the other hand, the work may, like most utopias, be interpreted as a negation of the present moment, the future paradise being constructed in order to reveal the crudeness of the time of writing. The work begins with Julian West's interesting description of his own society. He compares it to a carriage:

> By way of attempting to give the reader some general impression of the way people lived together in those days, and especially of the relations of the rich and poor to one another, perhaps I cannot do better than to compare society as it then was to a prodigious coach which the masses of humanity were harnessed to and dragged toilsomely along a very hilly and sandy road. The driver was hunger, and permitted no lagging, though the pace was necessarily very slow. Despite the difficulty of drawing the coach at all along so hard a road, the top was covered with passengers who never got down, even at the steepest ascents. These seats on top were very breezy and comfortable. Well up out of the dust, their occupants could enjoy the scenery at their leisure, or critically discuss the merits of the straining team. Naturally such places were in great demand and the competition for them was keen, every one seeking as the first end in life to secure a seat on the coach for himself and to leave it to his child after him.[11]

Bellamy's characterization is an apt, albeit cynical, description of western civilization in the nineteenth century. In spite of this, he seems to believe that inequality could be eradicated by peaceful means and that the widening gap between people would not lead to catastrophe, even though change was inevitable:

> The reader who observes the dates alluded to will of course recognize in these disturbances of industry the first and incoherent phase of the great movement which ended in the establishment of the modern

industrial system with all its social consequences. This is all so plain in the retrospect that a child can understand it, but not being prophets, we of that day had no clear idea what was happening to us. What we did see was that industrially the country was in a very queer way. The relation between the workingman and the employer, between labor and capital, appeared in some unaccountable manner to have become dislocated. The working classes had quite suddenly and very generally become infected with a profound discontent with their condition, and an idea that it could be greatly bettered if they only knew how to go about it. On every side, with one accord, they preferred demands for higher pay, shorter hours, better dwellings, better educational advantages, and a share in the refinements and luxuries of life, demands which it was impossible to see the way to granting unless the world were to become a great deal richer than it then was. Though they knew something of what they wanted, they knew nothing of how to accomplish it.[12]

By the end of the century it would no doubt have become clear to others as well as to Bellamy and his fictive Julian West that something had to happen. Demands for social change had increased, yet at the same time it was thought that equality was not economically feasible. In Bellamy's world, change came fairly late in the twentieth century through gradual improvement. But as he writes: 'This is all so plain in the retrospect . . .' The First World War and the subsequent socio-cultural changes were still unimaginable at the turn of the century. Ultimately, change was swift and violent. The war – and the October Revolution of 1917 – altered social conditions, and, in the process, also the imagination as well as visions of the future. After this rupture had taken place, the turn of the century was transformed into the *belle époque*, a lost world that was still innocently unaware of what the future would bring.

Notes

Introduction

1 Alfred de Musset, *Confession of a Child of the Century*, 11.

2 Clifford Geertz, *The Interpretation of Cultures: Selected Essays*, 3–30.

3 Mark Poster, 'The Question of Agency: Michel de Certeau and the History of Consumerism', 94.

4 Here I have to acknowledge my debt to the Finnish tradition of cultural history at the University of Turku. See, for example, Veikko Litzen, 'Kulttuurihistoria on kokonaisvaltaisuutta korostava historia', 7–17; Keijo Virtanen, *Kulttuurihistoria – tie kokonaisvaltaiseen historiaan*, 85; Kari Immonen, 'Uusi kulttuurihistoria', 20–5; Kirsi Tuohela and Anu Korhonen, 'Final Comments: Recoding Culture', 133–9.

5 See also Germán Arciniegas, *Kulturgeschichte Lateinamerikas*. Translated from the Spanish by Franz Damhort (Munich: Nymphenburger Verlag, 1966).

6 Wolfgang Schivelbusch, *The Railway Journey: Trains and Travel in the nineteenth Century*. Translated from the German by Anselm Hollo (Oxford: Blackwell, 1980).

7 Alfred de Musset, *Confession of a Child of the Century*, 7.

8 On the concept *fin de siècle*, see Mikuláš Teich and Roy Porter, 'Introduction', 1–9.

9   Armas J. Pulla, *Tammikuun ensimmäinen 1900*, 8–9.

10 Aino Ackté, *Muistojeni kirja*, 106.

11 Armas J. Pulla, *Tammikuun ensimmäinen 1900*, 8–9, 12–13.

12 Giuseppe Tomasi di Lampedusa, *The Leopard*, 181.

13 François-René de Chateaubriand, *Mémoires d'outre-tombe*, 382.

Chapter 1 Industrialization: Economy and Culture

1   Guy de Maupassant, *A Day in the Country and Other Stories*, 68.

2   In Spain industrialization started early but it proceeded slowly; see Adrian Shubert, *Social History of Modern Spain*, 8–9.

3   Geoff Eley, *Forging Democracy: The History of the Left in Europe, 1850–2000*, 48.

4   On Italy, see Maria Sophia Quine, *Italy's Social Revolution: Charity and Welfare from Liberalism to Fascism*, 28, 71. See also Nicholas V. Gianaris, *Geopolitical and Economic Changes in the Balkan Countries*, 44.

5   Eric J. Hobsbawm, 'The Machine Breakers', 62; Alun Howkins, 'Agrarian Histories and Agricultural Revolution', 81–2.

6   Adam Smith, *An Inquiry into the Nature and Causes of the Wealth of Nations*, 1–6.

7   Cf. an ironic commentary on Dumas's 'factory', in 'Letters and Impressions from Paris'. *Blackwood's Edinburgh Magazine* 60/372, October 1846, 417–18.

8   Victor Hugo, *Les Misérables*, 190.

9   Eric J. Hobsbawm, *The Age of Revolution 1789–1848*, 45.

10 John E. Archer, *Social Unrest and Popular Protest in England*, 46–7; W. Hamish Fraser, *History of British Trade Unionism, 1700–1988*, 16.

11 Hobsbawm, 'The Machine Breakers', 58–9.

12 Malcolm I. Thomis, *The Luddites. Machine-Breaking in Regency England*, 16; T. K. Derry and Trevor I. Williams, *A Short History of Technology from the Earliest Times to A. D. 1900*, 559; Samuel Lilley,' 'Technological Progress and the Industrial Revolution 1700–1914',192–3.

13 Thomis, op.cit., 11.

14 C. P. Hill, *British Economic and Social History, 1700–1982*, 61.

15 Thomis, op.cit., 59.

16 Eric J. Hobsbawm, *Industry and Empire*, 85.

17 Hobsbawm, 'The Machine Breakers', 58; Hill, op.cit., 67; Thomis, op.cit., 104.

18 Hobsbawm, *Industry and Empire*, 86.

19 Fraser, op.cit., 13–14, 25.

20 John Waller, *Real Oliver Twist*, 117–18, 349; Brian Lewis, *Middlemost and the Milltowns: Bourgeois Culture and Politics in Early Industrial England*, 104; Kim Lawes. *Paternalism and Politics: The Revival of Paternalism in Early Nineteenth-Century Britain*, 150–83.

21 William Wordsworth, *The Collected Poems of William Wordsworth*, 1037.

22 Cited in Hobsbawm, *Industry and Empire*, 86.

23 'Teollisuus', *Suomen Julkisia Sanomia*, 12 February 1857.

24 Charles Dickens, *Hard Times*, 27–8.

25 Lewis Mumford, *The Culture of Cities*, 196.

26 Lewis Mumford, *Technics and Civilization*, 285–7.

27 Herbert L. Sussman, *Victorians and the Machine: The Literary Response to Technology*, 1–5.

28 William Morris, *The Works of William Morris*, 3.

29 Friedrich Schiller, 'Über die ästhetische Erziehung des Menschen in einer Reihe von Briefen', 243–5.

30 William Blake, *The Complete Poetry and Prose of William Blake*, 228. See also Jacob Bronowski, *William Blake and the Age of Revolution*, 14–15.

31 Blake, op.cit., 159.

32 *Uusi Tietosanakirja*, 827. Translated by Kalle Pihlainen.

33 Hill, op.cit., 67; Brian Inglis, *Poverty and the Industrial Revolution*, 134–5.

34 George Gordon Byron, 'Parliamentary Speeches. Debate on the Frame-Work Bill, in the House of Lords, February 27, 1812', 676–7; R. C. Dallas, *Recollections of the Life of Lord Byron, from the Year 1808 to the End of 1814*, 208–9.

35 Krishan Kumar, *Utopia and Anti-Utopia in Modern Times*, 106–9.

36 Samuel Butler, *Erewhon, or Over the Range*, 263–8.

37 Kari Väyrynen, 'Omistusoikeus ja luonto: klassisen teorian ongelmia', 35–6.

38 Zachris Topelius, *Runoja*, 482. Translated by Kalle Pihlainen.

39 See Jouko Jokisalo, 'Ernst Rudorff, esteettinen sivilisaatiokritiikki ja Saksan luonnonsuojeluliikkeen alkukehitys', 16. The citation is from Ernst Rudorff's *Heimatschutz* (1901).

Chapter 2 The Faustian Man: A Society in Motion

1 Johann Wolfgang von Goethe, *Faust*, 11.

2 Stendhal, *The Red and the Black: a chronicle of 1830*, 236.

3 Sheryl Kroen, *Politics and Theater: The Crisis of Legitimacy in Restoration France, 1815–1830*, 202–3.

4 See, for example, Mary Wilson Carpenter, *Imperial Bibles, Domestic Bodies: Women, Sexuality and Religion in the Victorian Market*, xv–xxii; George Pattison, *Kierkegaard, Religion, and the Nineteenth-Century Crisis of Culture*, 129; Eleni Varikas, 'National and Gender Identity in Turn-of-the-Century Greece', 266–8; Jitka Malečková, 'The Emancipation of Women for the Benefit of the Nation: The Czech Women's Movement', 169–71.

5 Friedrich Engels's letter of 24 February 1893 to Danielson, cit. Edward Hallet Carr, *What Is History?*, 81.

6 Barry Millington, *Wagner*, 191–227.

7 K. E. Eurén, *Höyrykoneet. Niiden keksintö ja käytäntö*, 86.

8 Andrew Murray and Robert Murray, *Ship-building in Iron and Wood and Steam-ships*, 114–16.

9 Christopher McGowan, *Rail, Steam, and Speed: The Rocket and the Birth of Steam Locomotion*, 43–58. See also Francis Trevithick, *Life of Richard Trevithick: With an Account of His Inventions* (Cornwall: E. & F. N. Spon, 1872).

10 McGowan, *Rail, Steam, and Speed: The Rocket and the Birth of Steam Locomotion*, 1–31, 121–2.

11 William Bridges Adams, *English Pleasure Carriages; Their Origin, History, Varieties, Materials, Construction, Defects, Improvements, and Capabilities*, 198. The same quotation is used by Wolfgang Schivelbusch, *The Railway Journey. Trains and Travel in the nineteenth Century*, 17.

12 Leo Marx, *The Machine in the Garden: Technology and the Pastoral Ideal in America*, 196.

13 Op.cit., 196.

14 See, e.g., 'Ein Eisenbahndrama', *St Petersburger Zeitung*, 23 April/ 5 May 1853.

15 This may be ascertained by, for example, leafing through the 1853 issues of the *St Petersburger Zeitung*.

16 Raoul Palmgren, *Kaupunki ja tekniikka Suomen kirjallisuudessa: Kuvauslinjoja ennen ja jälkeen tulenkantajien*, 37.

17 Juhani Aho, 'Rautatie', 265–6.

18 Op.cit., 303.

19 Baedeker, *Paris and Its Environs:With Routes from London to Paris, and from Paris to the Rhine and Switzerland*, 277; Jean-Pierre A. Bernard, *Les deux Paris: les représentations de Paris dans la seconde moitié du XIXe siècle*, 147.

20 Allan Young, *Harmony of Illusions: Inventing Post-Traumatic Stress Disorder*, 5, 19–22. See also Lynne Kirby, 'Male Hysteria and Early Cinema', 118.

21 Ralph Harrington, 'The Railway Accident: Trains, Trauma, and Technological Crises in Nineteenth-Century Britain', 39.

22 Cited in Wolfgang Schivelbusch, *The Railway Journey. Trains and Travel in the nineteenth Century*, 139.

23 Cited in Wolfgang Schivelbusch, *The Railway Journey:Trains and Travel in the nineteenth Century*, 141.

24 Young, op.cit., 20; Kirby, op.cit., 116.

25 See, for example, Minna Uimonen, *Hermostumisen aikakausi: Neuroosit 1800- ja 1900-lukujen vaihteen suomalaisessa lääketieteessä*; Kirsi Tuohela, 'Being ill in the Past. Historicizing Women's Experience of Body and Illness', 46–68.

26 My observations are based on three newspapers, the *St Petersburger Zeitung* (St Petersburg), the *Svenska Tidningar* (Stockholm) and the *Åbo Tidningar* (Turku).

27 *St Petersburger Zeitung* (20 February/4 March 1853).

28 'Ångfartyget Lexingtons slutliga öde', *Åbo Tidningar* (9 November 1842).

29 Schivelbusch, *The Railway Journey. Trains and Travel in the nineteenth Century*, 44.

30 Heinrich Heine, *The Works of Heinrich Heine*, 368–9.

Chapter 3 From the Cult of Genius to Worship of Art

1 See, for example, Rohan McWilliam, *Popular Politics in Nineteenth-Century England*, 12, 66; Martin Conboy, *Journalism:A Critical History*, 88–127.

2 David Ferris, *Silent Urns: Romanticism, Hellenism, Modernity*, 16–107. See also Hannu Salmi, *Imagined Germany*.

3 François-René de Chateaubriand, *Atala – René*. A new translation by Irving Putter (Berkeley: University of California Press, 1980). See also David Wakefield, 'Chateaubriand's 'Atala' as a Source of Inspiration in Nineteenth-Century Art', 13–24.

4 Chateaubriand, *Atala – René*, 64–5.

5 For further detail, see Salmi, *Imagined Germany*, 53. Cf. Michael J. A. Howe, *Genius Explained*, 1.

6 Paul Metzner, *Crescendo of the Virtuoso: Spectacle, Skill, and Self-Promotion in Paris during the Age of Romanticism*, 124–36.

7 Heinrich Heine, *Florentine Nights*, 39–40.

8 See, for example, 'Notice physiologique. Sur Paganini.' *Revue de Paris* 26 (May 1831): 52–60; 'Paganini sorcier', *Le Figaro* (9 May 1831).

9 Heine, op.cit., 38.

10 Fr. Niecks, 'In Memoriam: Franz Liszt', *The Musical Times* 9 (1886); Heinrich Heine, 'Heinrich Heine's Musical Feuilletons', *The Musical Quarterly* 8/3 (July 1922): 458–9.

11 See, for example, Marcia Morse, 'Feminist Aesthetics and the Spectrum of Gender', *Philosophy East and West* 42/2 (April 1992): 287–95. Cf. Michael J. A. Howe, *Genius Explained*, 26.

12 Cited in Berthold Litzmann, *Clara Schumann: An Artist's Life* 1, 318–19. See also Nancy B. Reich, *Clara Schumann: The Artist and the Woman*, 2–3, 112, 175, 215.

13 Doris Starr Guilloton, 'Toward a New Freedom: Rahel Varnhagen and the German Women Writers before 1848', 133–44.

14 Marja Mustakallio, *'Teen nyt paljon musiikkia': Fanny Henselin (1805–1847) toiminta modernisoituvassa musiikkikulttuurissa*, 67–154. See also Marian Wilson Kimber, 'The 'Suppression' of Fanny Mendelssohn: Rethinking Feminist Biography', 113–29.

15 Marie-Hélène Huet, 'Chateaubriand and the Politics of (Im)mortality', 28–39.

16 Robert Baldick, 'Introduction', *Memoirs of Chateaubriand*, xvii.

17 Paganini's business methods were sharply commented on in the contemporary press. See, for example, 'L'Agent de Paganini', *Le Figaro* (5 December 1833).

18 'Heinrich Heine's Musical Feuilletons', *The Musical Quarterly* 8/3 (July 1922): 458.

19 Op.cit., 459.

20 R. Larry Todd, *Mendelssohn: A Life in Music*, 308–10.

21 J. H. Elliot, *Berlioz*, 185.

22 Amelita Marinetti, 'Death, Resurrection, and Fall in Dumas' Comte de Monte-Cristo', 260. See also *Histoire de la France littéraire* 3: 38.

23 Fredrika Bremer, *The Homes of the New World: Impressions of America*, vol. I–III. Translated by Mary Howitt (New York: Harper & Bros, 1853). See also Doris R. Asmundsson, 'Fredrika Bremer: Sweden's First Feminist', 99–110.

24 Rose-Marie Hagen and Rainer Hagen, *Goya: 1746–1828*, 54–63; Evan S. Connell, *Francisco Goya: A Life*, 156–8; Jutta Held, 'Francisco de Goya: Die Gemälde', 243–4.

25 See further, for example, Howard F. Isham, *Image of the Sea: Oceanic Consciousness in the Romantic Century*, 97–115.

26 'Heinrich Heine's Musical Feuilletons', *The Musical Quarterly* 8/3 (July 1922): 435.

27 Sixten Ringbom, 'Guérin, Delacroix and "The Liberty"', *The Burlington Magazine* 110/782 (May 1968): 270, 273–5.

28 Stephen Adams, *The Barbizon School and the Origins of Impressionism*, 63–226.

29 Joel Isaacson, 'Constable, Duranty, Mallarmé, Impressionism, Plein Air, and Forgetting', 427–50; Moshe Barasch, *Modern Theories of Art, 2. From Impressionism to Kandinsky*, 50.

30 David Carrier, 'Remembering the Past: Art Museums as Memory Theaters', *The Journal of Aesthetics and Art Criticism* 61/1 (winter 2003): 61–5.

31 Stendhal, *Rome, Naples and Florence*, 302.

32 Graziella Magherini, *La Sindrome di Stendhal* (Florence: Ponte Alle Grazie, 1989).

33 On the history of bibliomania, see Philip Connell, 'Bibliomania: Book Collecting, Cultural Politics, and the Rise of Literary Heritage in Romantic Britain', 24–47.

34 Stendhal, op.cit., 301.

35 Bayard Taylor, *Views A-Foot; or Europe. Seen with Knapsack and Staff*, 376–7.

36 George Stillman Hillard, *Six Months in Italy*, 88.

37 Cf. the special case of Rome in Taina Syrjämaa, *Constructing Unity, Living in Diversity: A Roman Decade*.

Chapter 4 On the Cultural History of Nationalism

1 Jeremy Jennings, 'The *Déclaration des droits de l'homme et du citoyen* and Its Critics in France: Reaction and *Idéologie*', 839–59.

2 Katherine B. Clinton, 'Femme et Philosophe: Enlightenment Origins of Feminism', 283–99; Gregory S. Brown, 'The Self-Fashionings of Olympe de Gouges, 1784–1789', 383–401.

3 Reinhart Koselleck et al., 'Volk, Nation, Nationalismus, Masse', 141–431.

4 On Gellner's theory, see Anthony D. Smith, *Nationalism and Modernism: A Critical Survey of Recent Theories of Nations and Nationalism*, 35–6.

5 Eric J. Hobsbawm, *Nations and Nationalism since 1780. Programme, Myth, Reality*, 8.

6 Benedict Anderson, *Imagined Communities*, 6.

7 Anthony D. Smith, *Nationalism: Theory, Ideology, History*, 97.

8 See closer Hannu Salmi, *Imagined Germany*, 41–2.

9 Hobsbawm, *Nations and Nationalism since 1780. Programme, Myth, Reality*, pp. 30–1, 101–30. See also Anthony D. Smith, *Nationalism and Modernism: A Critical Survey of Recent Theories of Nations and Nationalism*, 121.

10 See also Elías José Palti, 'The Nation as a Problem: Historians and the 'National Question'', 324–46.

11 Joseph von Eichendorff, *Life of a Good-for-nothing*, 11.

12 Dafydd R. Moore, 'The Critical Response to Ossian's Romantic Bequest', 38–53; Clare O'Halloran, 'Irish Re-Creations of the Gaelic Past: The Challenge of Macpherson's Ossian', 69–95.

13 Hannu Salmi, *Imagined Germany*, 38–40.

14 See further Matti Klinge, *Idylli ja uhka. Topeliuksen aatteita ja politiikkaa*, 278–313.

15 Zachris Topelius, *Välskärin kertomukset*, 3: 401.

16 Richard Wagner, *The Diary of Richard Wagner 1865–1882: The Brown Book*, 73.

17 See further Hannu Salmi, *Imagined Germany*, 52–61.

18 Richard Wagner, *Opera and Drama*, 178.

19 Hannu Salmi, *Imagined Germany*, 131–8.

20 Richard Wagner, *Die Meistersinger von Nürnberg – The Mastersingers of Nuremberg*. English translation of the libretto: Peter Branscombe. Deutsche Grammophon 415 278-2 (1985), 261.

21 Thomas S. Grey, 'Wagner's *Die Meistersinger* as National Opera (1868–1945)', 78–104; Dieter Borchmeyer, *Drama and the World of Richard Wagner*, 181–211.

22 Hannu Salmi, *Imagined Germany*, 136.
23 Karl Marx to Friedrich Engels, 19 August 1876, in Karl Marx and Friedrich Engels, *Gesamtausgabe*, 441.
24 Henry Bacon, *Oopperan historia*, 349–53.
25 Op.cit., 353–4. See also John A. Davis, 'Italy', 95–6.
26 Graham Scambler, *Sport and Society: History, Power and Culture*, 52–3; Arnd Krüger, 'The unfinished symphony: a history of the Olympic Games from Coubertin to Samaranch', 3–11; Jyrki Talonen, 'Poisjääntejä ja boikotteja olympialiikkeessä 1896–1984', 123–46.

Chapter 5 A Century of Family and Home: Daily Routines and Country Excursions

1 See, for example, Marianne Bernhard, *Das Biedermeier: Kultur zwischen Wiener Kongress und Märzrevolution*, 271.
2 Matti Klinge, *Kaukana ja kotona*, 131–7.
3 Anne Martin-Fugier, 'Les rites de la vie privée bourgeoise', *Histoire de la vie privée* 4: 215–27.
4 Kai Häggman, *Perheen vuosisata: Perheen ihanne ja sivistyneistön elämäntapa 1800-luvun Suomessa* (Helsinki: SKS, 1994).
5 Pirjo Markkola, *Työläiskodin synty: Tamperelaiset työläisperheet ja yhteiskunnallinen kysymys 1870-luvulta 1910-luvulle*, 126–30.
6 Anne Ollila, 'Questioning the Categories of Private and Public: Salons in the Nordic Countries in the Nineteenth Century', 125–31. See also Michelle Perrot, 'La vie de famille', *Histoire de la vie privée* 4: 187–91; Marjo Kaartinen, 'Public and Private: Challenges in the Study of Early Modern Women's Lives', 89–101.
7 Charles Dickens, *Oliver Twist*, 69.
8 Guy de Maupassant, *A Day in the Country and Other Stories*, 67–8.
9 Alain Corbin, *Time, Desire and Horror: Towards a History of the Senses*, see esp. chapter 'The Century of Linen'.
10 On Victorian consumer culture, see Lori Anne Loeb, *Consuming Angels: Advertising and Victorian Women*, vii–viii, 3–15.
11 Peter Ward, *Kitsch in Sync: A Consumer's Guide to Bad Taste*, 12. On the concept of *kitsch*, see Jukka Gronow, *Sociology of Taste*, 31–49.
12 Kari Kallioniemi, 'Porvarillisen populaarikulttuurin aikakausi', 51–6.
13 Martin-Fugier, op.cit., 199–215.
14 Thomas Mann, *Buddenbrooks: The Decline of a Family*, 29–30.

15 Martin-Fugier, op.cit., 199–215.

16 Martin-Fugier, op.cit., 199–208; Hanna Elomaa, 'Maalta kaupunkiin', 376, 386–8.

17 Anne Ollila, *Aika ja elämä:Aikakäsitys 1800-luvun lopussa*, 107–30.

18 Op.cit., 18–32, 107–30.

19 Elomaa, op.cit., 386.

20 Martin-Fugier, op.cit., 228–35. See also Orvar Löfgren, *On Holiday: A History of Vacationing*, 120.

21 For further detail, see Carola Rosengren, *Unelma kesästä: Huvilakulttuuria 1910-luvun Ruissalossa*.

22 Janne Ahtola, 'Britti-imperiumin siirtomaat matkakohteina 1800–1900-luvun vaihteessa', 64–81.

23 Guy de Maupassant, op.cit., 67.

24 Aleksander Pushkin, *The Queen of Spades and Other Stories*, 66–7.

25 Robert Darnton, 'History of Reading', 152; James Van Horn Melton, *Rise of the Public in Enlightenment Europe*. 111.

26 Gustave Flaubert, *Madame Bovary*, 116–17.

27 Anu Koivunen, 'Näkyvä nainen ja 'suloinen pyörrytys': Naiset tähtinä ja tähtien kuluttajina 1920-luvun suomalaisessa elokuvajournalismissa', 190–1.

28 Cosima Wagner's diary entries on 10 January 1872, 16 February and 18 February 1876, in Cosima Wagner, *Diaries*, 1: 448, 893, and diary entry on 23 January 1881, in Cosima Wagner, *Diaries*, 2: 606.

29 Alain Corbin, 'Le secret de l'individu', 486–9.

30 For further detail, see Andreas Ballstaedt and Tobias Widmaier, *Salonmusik: Zur Geschichte und Funktion einer bürgerlichen Musikpraxis*, 34–8, 60–79. See also Hannu Salmi, *Wagner and Wagnerism in Nineteenth-Century Sweden, Finland, and the Baltic Provinces: Reception, Enthusiasm, Cult*, 34–44.

31 Martin-Fugier, op.cit., 208–15.

32 On Parisian opera, see Anselm Gerhard, *The Urbanization of Opera: Music Theater in Paris in the Nineteenth Century*, 1–40, 158–214.

33 Gustave Flaubert, op.cit., 49–50.

34 Alain Corbin, 'Le secret de l'individu', 446–50.

35 See, for example, Matti Klinge, *Kaukana ja kotona*, 121–31; Anne Ollila, *Jalo velvollisuus: Virkanaisena 1800-luvun lopun Suomessa*; Irma Sulkunen, 'Naisten järjestäytyminen ja kaksijakoinen kansalaisuus', 157–72.

Chapter 6 Baudelaire in the Department Store: Urban Living and Consumption

1 Charles Baudelaire, *Paris Spleen*, 20.
2 Originally 'Crowds' had, however, appeared in the journal *Revue fantaisiste* in 1861.
3 Op.cit., 15.
4 Kenneth Pomeranz, *Great Divergence: China, Europe and the Making of the Modern World Economy*, 13.
5 'Beau Brummell', *The Times* (7 January 1830).
6 Marylène Delbourg-Delphis. *Masculin singulier. Le dandysme et son histoire*, 15–25. See also 'El conde Alfredo de Orsay'. *Museo de las familias* (25 February 1853).
7 'Album de la Iberia. Correspondencia de Paris.' *La Iberia* (30 August 1859).
8 Declan Kiberd, 'Anarchist Attitudes: Oscar Wilde', 40–51. See also David Schulz, 'Redressing Oscar: Performance and the Trials of Oscar Wilde', 37–59.
9 Delbourg-Delphis, op.cit., 154–65.
10 Delbourg-Delphis, op.cit., 154–9. See also Declan Kiberd, 'Anarchist Attitudes: Oscar Wilde', 50–1; 'El proceso Wilde.' *La Dinastia* (13 April 1895).
11 See, for example, David Frisby, 'The *flâneur* in social theory', 81–3.
12 Charles Baudelaire, *Les Fleurs du Mal*, 32.
13 Charles Baudelaire, *Selected Writings on Art and Literature*, 399, 400–1.
14 Ibid., 400.
15 See further Wolfgang Schivelbusch, *Disenchanted Night. The Industrialization of Light in the Nineteenth Century*. See also Jill Harsin, *Barricades: The War of the Streets in Revolutionary Paris, 1830–1848*, 85.
16 Baudelaire, *Paris Spleen*, 108.
17 Anne Friedberg, *Window Shopping: Cinema and the Postmodern*, 32–7.
18 Op.cit., 47–94.
19 Anne Higonnet, 'Real Fashion: Clothes Unmake the Working Woman', 157.
20 Émile Zola, *The Ladies' Paradise: A Realistic Novel*, 208. Quoted in Friedberg, op.cit., 42.
21 Heide Schlüppmann, 'Kinosucht', 45–52. See also Miriam Hansen, 'Early Silent Cinema: Whose Public Sphere?', 147–84.

22　Friedberg, op.cit., 38–9.

23　Georg Simmel, *The Philosophy of Money*, 433.

Chapter 7　The Breakthrough of Mechanical Reproduction

1　Georges Méliès, 'Cinematographic Views' (1907), 36–7.

2　Erkki Huhtamo, 'Ennen broadcastingia', 6–17; Erkki Huhtamo, *Fantasmagoria: Elävän kuvan arkeologiaa*, 96–7. See also Erkki Huhtamo, 'From Kaleidoscomaniac to Cybernerd: Notes toward an Archaeology of the Media,' 221–4.

3　David Brewster, *Stereoscope. Its History, Theory, and Construction*, 31, 36.

4　Huhtamo, 'Ennen broadcastingia', 6–17.

5　Malcolm Daniel, '"Divine Perfection": The Daguerreotype in Europe and America', 41.

6　Irma Savolainen, *Taiteilijoita, käsityöläisiä ja taivaanrannanmaalareita: Turkulaiset valokuvaajat vuoteen 1918*, 10.

7　Op.cit., 92–3.

8　Alain Corbin,'Le secret de l'individu', 421–3.

9　Savolainen, op.cit., 112–13.

10　Anne Friedberg, *Window Shopping: Cinema and the Postmodern*, 25–6, 41. See also Vanessa R. Schwartz, *Spectacular Realities: Early Mass Culture in Fin-de-Siècle Paris*, 149–76.

11　Hannu Salmi, *'Atoomipommilla kuuhun!' Tekniikan mentaalihistoriaa*, 141.

12　David Livingstone, *Livingstone's Travels and Researches in South Africa*, 139.

13　See, for example, Huhtamo, *Fantasmagoria: Elävän kuvan arkeologiaa*, 126. See also Gian Piero Brunetta, *Cent'anni di cinema italiano*, 1: 1–19.

14　For further detail, see Bob Rose, 'Projection', 804–5; Josh Marsh, 'Spectacle', 276–8.

15　Georges Sadoul, *Georges Méliès*, 56.

16　*Uusi Suometar* (28 June 1896).

17　See, for example, Erkki Huhtamo, 'From Kaleidoscomaniac to Cybernerd: Notes toward an Archaeology of the Media,' 224. The early film has been published in the *Early Cinema* collection by the British Film Institute.

18　Susan Larson and Eva Woords, 'Visualizing Spanish Modernity: Introduction', 9.

19 Tom Gunning, 'An Aesthetic of Astonishment: Early Film and the (In)credulous Spectator', 79.

20 Ibid., 78–95. See also John Docker, *Postmodernism and Popular Culture: A Cultural History*, 71; Scott McQuire, *Visions of Modernity: Representation, Memory, Time and Space in the Age of the Camera*, 64.

21 *Uusi Suometar* (28 June 1896).

22 'Mr. Edison', *The Times* (31 December 1878).

23 Pekka Gronow and Ilpo Saunio, *An International History of the Record Industry*, 8–35. See also Th. du Moncel, 'Sur le phonographe de M. Edison', 643–5.

24 See, for example, 'Mr. Edison', *The Times* (31 December 1878); 'Crónica de la semana', *El semanario murciano* (29 September 1878); *Helsingfors Dagblad* (18 August 1878); 'Fonografens uppfinnare', *Morgonbladet* (12 July 1878); Claës Lundin, *Oxygen och Aromasia*, 7–8.

25 Zachris Topelius, *Sånger* 3: 272– 3. Translated by Kalle Pihlainen.

26 *Uusi Suometar* (17 April 1904). Quoted in Sven Hirn, *Kuvat kulkevat: Kuvallisten esitysten perinne ja elävien kuvien 12 ensimmäistä vuotta Suomessa*, 179.

27 Pekka Gronow and Ilpo Saunio, *An International History of the Record Industry*, 8–35.

28 Ibid., 10–11.

Chapter 8   Colonial Culture and European Identity

1 Georg Wilhelm Friedrich Hegel, *Vorlesungen über die Philosophie der Weltgeschichte*, 232–47.

2 The term 'imperialism' can, of course, be used in other ways. It is often used as a means of criticism with the intention of belittling a political opponent (e.g. 'Western imperialism in the Third World' or 'American imperialism in Vietnam'). Lenin used 'imperialism' to signify the 'highest form of capitalism' in which world economy was controlled by monopolies.

3 Janne Ahtola, 'Britti-imperiumin siirtomaat matkakohteina 1800– 1900-luvun vaihteessa', 64–5.

4 *Charles Darwin's Beagle Diary*, 446.

5 Jules Verne, *Five Weeks in a Balloon*, 123.

6 On Jules Verne's technophilia, see Paul K. Alkon, *Science Fiction Before 1900. Imagination Discovers Technology*, 56–100.

7 On transculturation, see Peter Burke, *Varieties of Cultural History*, 207–8.

8 See, for example, Anne McClintock, *Imperial Leather: Race, Gender and Sexuality in the Colonial Contest*, 21–74.

9 Rudyard Kipling, *Complete Verse*, 321.

10 Op.cit., 322.

11 Rudyard Kipling, *The Jungle Book*.

12 Joseph Conrad, *Heart of Darkness*, 65.

13 Kipling, *Complete Verse*, 404.

14 See closer Salmi, *Imagined Germany*, 43.

15 J. W. Burrow, *The Crisis of Reason: European Thought, 1848–1914*, 106–8.

16 On the problem of otherness, see Marjo Kaartinen, 'Toinen – vieras. Näkökulmia kolonialistisen toiseuden tutkimukseen', 387–401.

17 Edward W. Said, *Orientalism*. See also Bill Ashcroft and Pal Ahluwalia, *Edward Said*, 49–84.

18 On travel accounts, see Leila Koivunen, *Visualizing Africa in Nineteenth-Century British Travel Accounts*.

19 Kari Kallioniemi, 'Porvarillisen populaarikulttuurin aikakausi', 49–50.

20 Cited in Penny Summerfield, 'Patriotism and Empire: Music-Hall Entertainment 1870-1914', 17–48.

21 David Mayer, 'Introduction', 1–22.

22 Anne E. Coombes, *Reinventing Africa: Museums, Material Culture and Popular Imagination in Late Victorian and Edwardian England*, 63–83.

23 Auvo Kostiainen, 'Massaturismin historiallinen syntymä', 16; Fred Inglis, *Delicious History of the Holiday*, 14, 47, 71.

24 Janne Ahtola, 'Britti-imperiumin siirtomaat matkakohteina 1800–1900-luvun vaihteessa', 64–81; Janne Ahtola, 'Thomas Cook & Son – perheyrityksenä maailmankartalle', 39–65; Inglis, *Delicious History of the Holiday*, 47–9.

25 Schliemann's own account on the excavations was published in English in 1875. See Heinrich Schliemann, *Troy and Its Remains: A Narrative of Researches and Discoveries Made on the Site of Ilium, and in the Trojan Plain* (London: J. Murray, 1875). See also 'Troy', *The Times* (31 March 1875).

26 For further detail, see Donald Malcolm Reid, *Whose Pharaohs?: Archaeology, Museums and Egyptian Identity from Napolean to World War I*, 139–285.

27 See, for example, Suzanne Marchand, 'Ancients and Moderns in German Museums', 186–9.

Chapter 9 Fin de Siècle: *The End of a Century*

1 Mikuláš Teich and Roy Porter, 'Introduction', 1–9.
2 Lois N. Magner, *A History of the Life Sciences*, 243–50; David A. Barnes, *Great Stink of Paris and the Nineteenth-Century Struggle Against Filth and Germs*, 1–2.
3 Barnes, op.cit., 1–2.
4 J. W. Burrow, *The Crisis of Reason: European Thought, 1848–1914*, 42–52.
5 Charles Darwin, *On the Origin of Species by Means of Natural Selection, or the Preservation of Favoured Races in the Struggle for Life*, 458–9.
6 J. W. Burrow, op.cit., 92–6.
7 Dieter Borchmeyer, 'Richard Wagner und der Antisemitismus', 137–8.
8 Op.cit., 139–40.
9 Robert Louis Stevenson, *The Strange Case of Dr Jekyll and Mr Hyde*, 51.
10 Alain Corbin, 'Le secret de l'individu', 430–6; Tapio Onnela, 'Kuvaan kiinnittyvä valta: Valokuvaus tiedon ja kontrollin kentässä', 19–28.
11 Stevenson, op.cit., 50.
12 L. Perry Curtis Jr., *Jack the Ripper and the London Press*, 109–275. See also Christopher Frayling, 'The House That Jack Built: Some Stereotypes of the Rapist in the History of Popular Culture', 174–215.
13 On Freud's early career, see Lars Sjögren, *Sigmund Freud: Elämä ja teokset*, 14–19, 46–70.
14 Sjögren, op.cit., 71–95. See also Sigmund Freud, *The Interpretation of Dreams*, 38–42, 155–7.
15 Sigmund Freud, *Three Essays on the Theory of Sexuality*, 39–69. See also Joseph Bristow, *Sexuality*, 64–5.
16 Sjögren, op.cit., 128.
17 Kirsi Tuohela, 'Being ill in the Past: Historicizing Women's Experience of Body and Illness'; Minna Uimonen, *Hermostumisen aikakausi: Neuroosit 1800- ja 1900-lukujen vaihteen suomalaisessa lääketieteessä*; Ritva Hapuli, *Nykyajan sininen kukka: Olavi Paavolainen ja nykyaika*, 117; Alain Corbin, 'Cris et chuchotements', 568–70; Athena. Vrettos, *Somatic Fictions: Imagining Illness in Victorian Culture*, 48–80.

18 On Dora's case, see Sjögren, op.cit., 96–107; Hannah S. Decker, 'Freud's "Dora" Case: The Crucible of the Psychoanalytic Concept of Transference', 105–16.

19 Declan Kiberd, 'Anarchist Attitudes: Oscar Wilde', 49–51; Marylène Delbourg-Delphis, *Masculin singulier: Le dandysme et son histoire*, 140–65. On decadence, see Burrow, op.cit., 182–7.

20 Erwin Koppen, 'Wagnerismus – Begriff und Phänomen', 617–20; Burrow, op.cit., 182–7.

21 Koppen, op.cit., 617–18; Burrow, op.cit., 184–5. See also Charles Bernheimer, *Decadent Subjects: The Idea of Decadence in Art, Literature, Philosophy, and Culture of the Fin de Siècle in Europe*, 7–33, 58, 71–3.

22 On Verne's career, see Paul K. Alkon, *Science Fiction Before 1900: Imagination Discovers Technology*, 65–7.

23 Jules Verne, *Five Weeks in a Balloon*, 123.

24 Jules Verne, *Robur the Conqueror*, 158.

25 For further detail, see Hannu Salmi, *'Atoomipommilla kuuhun!' Tekniikan mentaalihistoriaa*, 126–30.

26 Jules Verne, *Robur the Conqueror*, 159.

27 Jules Verne, *Master of the World*, 25.

28 On occultism, see Burrow, op.cit., 219–33.

29 Arthur Conan Doyle, *The Hound of the Baskervilles*, 111–12.

30 *Helsingin Sanomat* (18 April 1912).

Chapter 10 Conclusion: 'Things to Come'

1 Paul K. Alkon, *Science Fiction Before 1900: Imagination Discovers Technology*, 21. On Mercier, see Riikka Forsström, *Possible Worlds: The Idea of Happiness in the Utopian Vision of Louis-Sébastien Mercier*.

2 Heli Paalumäki, '"Imagine a Good Day" – Bertrand de Jouvenel's Idea of Possible Futures in the Context of Fictitious and Historical Narratives', 1–9.

3 See, for example, Hannu Salmi, *Imagined Germany*, 69–80.

4 Jules Verne, *Paris in the Twentieth Century*, 96.

5 Claës Lundin, *Oxygen och Aromasia*, 7–8. The citation has been translated into English by Keith Battarbee.

6 On the influence of *The Time Machine*, see Alkon, op.cit., 41–55. See also J. R. Hammond, '*The Time Machine* as a First Novel: Myth and Allegory in Wells's Romance', 3–11.

7 H. G. Wells, *The Time Machine*, 62.
8 Wells, op.cit., 62–3.
9 Wells, op.cit., 62–3.
10 For further details, see Alkon, op.cit., 107–15.
11 Edward Bellamy, *Looking Backward, 2000–1887*, 7.
12 Op.cit., 11.

Bibliography

Contemporary Literature

Ackté, Aino. *Muistojeni kirja*. Helsinki: Otava, 1925.

Adams, William Bridges. *English Pleasure Carriages: Their Origin, History, Varieties, Materials, Construction, Defects, Improvements, and Capabilities.* London: Charles Knight & Co., 1837.

Aho, Juhani. 'Rautatie' (1884). In *Kootut teokset*. Vol. 1. Porvoo: WSOY, 1918.

Baedeker. *Paris and Its Environs: With Routes from London to Paris, and from Paris to the Rhine and Switzerland.* Sixth edition. Leipzig: K. Baedeker, 1878.

Baudelaire, Charles. *Les Fleurs du Mal.* The new English translation by Richard Howard. Boston: David R. Godine, 1983.

Baudelaire, Charles. *Paris Spleen.* Translated from the French by Louise Varèse. New York: New Directions, 1970.

Baudelaire, Charles. *Selected Writings on Art and Literature.* Translated with an Introduction by P. E. Charvet. Harmondsworth: Penguin, 1992.

Bellamy, Edward. *Looking Backward, 2000–1887* (1888). With an Introduction by Walter James Miller. New York: Signet Classic, 2000.

Blake, William. *The Complete Poetry and Prose of William Blake.* Edited by David V. Erdman. Commentary by Harold Bloom. New and revised edition. Berkeley: University of California Press, 1982.

Bremer, Fredrika. *The Homes of the New World: Impressions of America*, Vol. I–III. Translated by Mary Howitt. New York: Harper & Bros, 1853.

Brewster, David. *Stereoscope. Its History, Theory, and Construction*. London: John Murray, 1856.

Butler, Samuel. *Erewhon, or Over the Range* (1872). London: Jonathan Cape, 1947.

Byron, George Gordon. 'Parliamentary Speeches. Debate on the Frame-Work Bill, in the House of Lords, February 27, 1812.' In Thomas Moore, *Life of Lord Byron, with His Letters and Journals*. London: John Murray, 1851.

Conrad, Joseph. *Heart of Darkness* (1902). Cheswold, Delaware: Prestwick House, 2004.

Dallas, R. C. *Recollections of the Life of Lord Byron, from the Year 1808 to the End of 1814*. Taken from authentic documents in the possession of the author. London: Charles Knight, 1824.

Darwin, Charles. *On the Origin of Species by Means of Natural Selection, or the Preservation of Favoured Races in the Struggle for Life*. Cambridge, Mass.: Harvard University Press, 1964.

Darwin, Charles. *Charles Darwin's Beagle Diary*. Edited by R. D. Keynes. Cambridge: Cambridge University Press, 2001.

de Chateaubriand, François-René. *Memoirs of Chateaubriand*. Selected, translated and with an introduction by Robert Baldick. London: Hamish Hamilton, 1961.

de Chateaubriand, François-René. *Atala – René*. A new translation by Irving Putter. Berkeley: University of California Press, 1980.

de Chateaubriand, François-René. *Mémoires d'outre-tombe*. Books I–XII. Edited by Jean-Claude Berchet. Paris: Garnier, 1989.

de Maupassant, Guy. *A Day in the Country and Other Stories*. Translated with an Introduction and Notes by David Coward. Oxford: Oxford University Press, 1998.

de Musset, Alfred. *Confession of a Child of the Century*. Crowned by the French Academy. With a preface by Henri de Bonier, of the French Academy. First published in 1910. New York: Howard Fertig, 1977.

Dickens, Charles. *Hard Times* (1854). Edited with an Introduction and Notes by Kate Flint. London: Penguin, 2003.

Dickens, Charles. *Oliver Twist*. London: Chapman & Hall, 1897.

Doyle, Arthur Conan. *The Hound of the Baskervilles* (1902). New York: Signet Classic, 2001.

Eichendorff, Joseph von. *Life of a Good-for-nothing*. Translated by J. G. Nichols. London: Hesperus Press, 2002.

Eurén, K. E. *Höyrykoneet. Niiden keksintö ja käytäntö*. Hämeenlinna: Eurén, 1863.

Flaubert, Gustave. *Madame Bovary: Provincial Lives* (1857). Translated with an Introduction and Notes by Geoffrey Wall. Preface by Michèle Roberts. London: Penguin, 2003.

Freud, Sigmund. *The Interpretation of Dreams* (1899). Translated by A. A. Brill. Introduction by Stephen Wilson. Hertfordshire, Wordsworth Editions, 1997.

Freud, Sigmund. *Three Essays on the Theory of Sexuality* (1905). With a new foreword by Nancy J. Chodorow. Introductory essay by Steven Marcus. Translated by James Strachey. New York: Basic Books, 2000.

Goethe, Johann Wolfgang von. *Faust*. Translated by George Madison Priest. Chicago: Encyclopædia Britannica, 1952.

Hegel, Georg Wilhelm Friedrich. *Vorlesungen über die Philosophie der Weltgeschichte*. Sämtliche Werke, Band VIII. Erster Halbband. Hrsg. von Georg Lasson. Leipzig: Meiner, 1920.

Heine, Heinrich. *The Works of Heinrich Heine*. Translated by Charles Godfrey Leland. London: W. Heinemann, 1893.

Heine, Heinrich. 'Heinrich Heine's Musical Feuilletons'. *The Musical Quarterly* 8/3 (July 1922): 458–9.

Heine, Heinrich. *Florentine Nights*. Translated by Kirke Boyle Fitzgerald. Boston: The Christopher Publishing House, 1929.

Hillard, George Stillman. *Six Months in Italy*. Sixth edition. Boston: Ticknor and Fields, 1860.

Hugo, Victor. *Les Misérables*. Volume I: *Fantine*. Translator Isabel F. Hapgood. New York: Thomas Y. Crowell & Co, 1887.

Kipling, Rudyard. *The Jungle Book* (1894–5). London: Macmillan, 1955.

Kipling, Rudyard. *Complete Verse*. Definitive edition. New York: Anchor, 1988.

Livingstone, David. *Livingstone's Travels and Researches in South Africa*. Philadelphia: J. W. Bradley, 1860.

Lundin, Claës. *Oxygen och Aromasia*. Stockholm: Seligmann & Co, 1878.

Mann, Thomas. *Buddenbrooks: The Decline of a Family* (1901). Translated from the German by H. T. Lowe-Porter. Harmondsworth: Penguin, 1982.

Marx, Karl and Engels, Friedrich. *Gesamtausgabe*. Part 3, Vol. 4: *Der*

Briefwechsel zwischen Marx und Engels 1868–1883. Berlin: Dietz, 1931.

Méliès, Georges. 'Cinematographic Views' (1907), in Richard Abel, *French Film Theory and Criticism: A History/Anthology, 1907–1939.* Princeton: Princeton University Press, 1988.

Moncel, Th. du. 'Sur le phonographe de M. Edison'. *Académie des sciences: Comptes rendus hebdomadaires des séances de l'Académie des sciences,* 643–5. Paris: Académies des sciences, 1878.

Morris, William. *The Works of William Morris.* Third volume. Edited by May Morris. London: Longmans, 1910–15.

Murray, Andrew and Murray, Robert. *Ship-building in Iron and Wood and Steam-ships.* Second edition. Edinburgh: Adam and Charles Black, 1863.

Niecks, Fr. 'In Memoriam: Franz Liszt'. *The Musical Times* 9 (1886).

Pushkin, Aleksandr. *The Queen of Spades and Other Stories.* Translated from the Russian by T. Keane. New York: Dover Publications, 1994.

Schiller, Friedrich: 'Über die ästhetische Erziehung des Menschen in einer Reihe von Briefen' (1795). In *Schillers Werke in drei Bänden.* Edited by Reinhard Buchwald. Vol. 2. Leipzig: Insel, 1941.

Schliemann, Heinrich. *Troy and Its Remains: A Narrative of Researches and Discoveries Made on the Site of Ilium, and in the Trojan Plain.* Translated by L. Dora Schmitz. London: J. Murray, 1875.

Simmel, Georg. *The Philosophy of Money.* Translated by Tom Bottomore and David Frisby. London: Routledge & Kegan Paul, 1978.

Smith, Adam. *An Inquiry into the Nature and Causes of the Wealth of Nations* (1776). With a life of the author, an introductory discourse, notes, and supplement dissertation by J. R. McCulloch, Esq. Edinburgh: Adam and Charles Black, 1863.

Stendhal. *Rome, Naples and Florence.* Translated by Richard N. Coe. New York: George Braziller, Inc., 1960.

Stendhal. *The Red and the Black: A Chronicle of 1830.* Translated by Charles Tergie. Franklin Center, Pa.: Franklin Library, 1984.

Stevenson, Robert Louis. *The Strange Case of Dr Jekyll and Mr Hyde* (1886). Raleigh, North Carolina: Hayes Barton Press, 2007.

Taylor, Bayard. *Views A-Foot; or Europe. Seen with Knapsack and Staff.* New York: G. P. Putnam, 1862.

Tomasi di Lampedusa, Giuseppe: *The Leopard.* Translated from the Italian by Archibald Colquhoun with an Introduction by David Gilmour. London: David Campbell Publishers, 1998.

Topelius, Zachris. *Sånger. Vol. 3*. Helsinki: Edlunds, 1905.

Topelius, Zachris. *Runoja*. Fourth edition. Porvoo: WSOY, 1949.

Topelius, Zachris. *Välskärin kertomukset, Vol. 3*. Translated by Juhani Aho. Porvoo: WSOY, 1974.

Trevithick, Francis. *Life of Richard Trevithick: With an Account of His Inventions*. Cornwall: E. & F. N. Spon, 1872.

Uusi Tietosanakirja. Vol. 3. Helsinki: Tietosanakirja, 1966.

Verne, Jules. *The Master of the World* (1904). Gloucester: Dodo Press, 2005.

Verne, Jules. *Paris in the Twentieth Century*. Translated by Richard Howard. Introduction by Eugen Weber. New York: Random House, 1996.

Verne, Jules. *Robur the Conqueror* (1886). Gloucester: Dodo Press, 2005.

Verne, Jules. *Five Weeks in a Balloon* (1863). Translated by William Lackland. West Stockbridge, MA: Hard Press, 2006.

Wagner, Cosima. *Diaries*. Edited and annotated by Martin Gregor-Dellin and Dietrich Mack. Translated by Geoffrey Skelton. Vol. 1: 1869–77. Vol. 2: 1878–83. London: Collins, 1978–80.

Wagner, Richard. *The Diary of Richard Wagner 1865–1882. The Brown Book*. Presented and annotated by Joachim Bergfeld. Translated by George Byrd. Cambridge: Cambridge University Press, 1980.

Wagner, Richard. *Die Meistersinger von Nürnberg – The Mastersingers of Nuremberg*. English translation of the libretto: Peter Branscombe. Deutsche Grammophon 415 278-2 (1985).

Wagner, Richard: *Opera and Drama*. Richard Wagner's Prose Works. Vol. 2. Translated by William Ashton Ellis. London: Kegan, Paul, Trench, Trubner & Co,. 1893; reprint, Lincoln: University of Nebraska Press, 1995.

Wells, H. G. *The Time Machine*. Bloomington: Indiana University Press, 1987.

Wordsworth, William. *The Collected Poems of William Wordsworth*. With an Introduction by Antonia Till. Hertfordshire, Wordsworth Editions, 1995.

Zola, Émile. *The Ladies' Paradise: A Realistic Novel*. London: Vizetelly, 1886.

Newspapers

Åbo Tidningar, Turku 1842.

Blackwood's Edinburgh Magazine, Edinburgh 1846.

Dinastia, La, Barcelona 1895.

Figaro, Le, Paris 1831–1834.
Helsingfors Dagblad, Helsinki 1878.
Helsingin Sanomat, Helsinki 1912.
Iberia, La, Madrid 1859.
Morgonbladet, Helsinki 1878.
Museo de las familias, Madrid 1853.
Revue de Paris, Paris 1831.
St Petersburger Zeitung, St Petersburg 1853.
Semanario murciano, El, Murcia 1878.
Suomen Julkisia Sanomia, Helsinki 1857.
Svenska Tidningar, Stockholm. 1840–59
Times, The, London 1830, 1875, 1878.
Uusi Suometar, Helsinki 1896, 1904.

Research Literature

Adams, James Eli. 'Victorian Sexualities'. In *A Companion to Victorian Literature and Culture.* Edited by Herbert F. Tucker, 125–40. Oxford: Blackwell, 1999.

Adams, Stephen. *The Barbizon School and the Origins of Impressionism.* London: Phaidon Press, 1997.

Ahtola, Janne. 'Thomas Cook & Son – perheyrityksenä maailmankartalle'. In *Matkakuumetta. Matkailun ja turismin historiaa.* Edited by Taina Syrjämaa. Turku: University of Turku, Department of History, 1994.

Ahtola, Janne. 'Britti-imperiumin siirtomaat matkakohteina 1800–1900-luvun vaihteessa'. In *Mikä maa, mikä valuutta: Matkakirja turismin historiaan.* Edited by Auvo Kostiainen and Katariina Korpela. Turku: University of Turku, Department of History, 1995.

Alkon, Paul K. *Science Fiction Before 1900: Imagination Discovers Technology.* Twayne's Studies in Literary Themes and Genres No. 3. New York: Twayne, 1994.

Anderson, Benedict. *Imagined Communities. Reflections on the Origin and Spread of Nationalism.* Revised edition. 7th impr. London: Verso, 1996.

Archer, John E. *Social Unrest and Popular Protest in England.* Cambridge: Cambridge University Press, 2000.

Arciniegas, Germán. *Kulturgeschichte Lateinamerikas.* Translated from the Spanish by Franz Damhort. Munich: Nymphenburger Verlag, 1966.

Ashcroft, Bill and Ahluwalia, Pal. *Edward Said*. London: Routledge, 2000.

Asmundsson, Doris R. 'Fredrika Bremer: Sweden's First Feminist'. In *Woman as Mediatrix: Essays on Nineteenth-Century European Women Writers*. Vol. 10. Edited by Avriel H. Goldberger, 99–110. New York: Greenwood Press, 1987.

Bacon, Henry. *Oopperan historia*. Helsinki: Otava, 1995.

Baldick, Robert. 'Introduction'. In *Memoirs of Chateaubriand*. Selected, translated and with an introduction by Robert Baldick. London: Hamish Hamilton, 1961.

Ballstaedt, Andreas and Widmaier, Tobias. *Salonmusik: Zur Geschichte und Funktion einer bürgerlichen Musikpraxis*. Stuttgart: Steiner, 1989.

Barasch, Moshe. *Modern Theories of Art, 2. From Impressionism to Kandinsky*. New York: New York University Press, 1998.

Barnes, David A. *Great Stink of Paris and the Nineteenth-Century Struggle Against Filth and Germs*. Baltimore, Maryland: The Johns Hopkins University Press, 2006.

Bernard, Jean-Pierre A. *Les deux Paris: les représentations de Paris dans la seconde moitié du XIXe siècle*. Seyssel: Éditions Chapm Vallon, 2001.

Bernhard, Marianne. *Das Biedermeier: Kultur zwischen Wiener Kongress und Märzrevolution*. Düsseldorf: Econ Verlag, 1983.

Bernheimer, Charles. *Decadent Subjects: The Idea of Decadence in Art, Literature, Philosophy, and Culture of the Fin de Siècle in Europe*. Edited by T. Jefferson Kline and Naomi Schor. Baltimore: The Johns Hopkins University Press, 2002.

Borchmeyer, Dieter. 'Richard Wagner und der Antisemitismus'. In *Richard-Wagner-Handbuch*. Edited by Ulrich Müller and Peter Wapnewski. Stuttgart: Kröner, 1986.

Borchmeyer, Dieter. *Drama and the World of Richard Wagner*. Translated by Daphne Ellis. Princeton: Princeton University Press, 2003.

Bristow, Joseph. *Sexuality*. London: Routledge, 1997.

Bronowski, Jacob. *William Blake and the Age of Revolution*. London: Routledge & Kegan Paul, 1972.

Brown, Gregory S. 'The Self-Fashionings of Olympe de Gouges, 1784-1789'. *Eighteenth-Century Studies* 34/3, French Revolutionary Culture (spring 2001): 383–401.

Brunetta, Gian Piero. *Cent'anni di cinema italiano*. Vol. 1. Rome: Editori Laterza, 2004.

Burke, Peter. *Varieties of Cultural History*. Cambridge: Polity, 1997.

Burrow, J. W. *The Crisis of Reason: European Thought, 1848–1914*. New Haven: Yale University Press, 2000.

Carpenter, Mary Wilson. *Imperial Bibles, Domestic Bodies: Women, Sexuality and Religion in the Victorian Market*. Athens, Ohio: Ohio University Press, 2003.

Carr, Edward Hallet. *What is History?* (1961). Harmondsworth: Penguin, 1986.

Carrier, David. 'Remembering the Past: Art Museums as Memory Theaters'. *The Journal of Aesthetics and Art Criticism* 6/1 (winter 2003): 61–5.

Clinton, Katherine B. 'Femme et Philosophe: Enlightenment Origins of Feminism'. *Eighteenth-Century Studies* 8/3 (spring 1975): 283–99.

Conboy, Martin. *Journalism: A Critical History*. London: Sage, 2004.

Connell, Evan S. *Francisco Goya: A Life*. New York: Counterpoint, 2004.

Connell, Philip. 'Bibliomania: Book Collecting, Cultural Politics, and the Rise of Literary Heritage in Romantic Britain'. *Representations* 71 (summer 2000): 24–47.

Coombes, Annie E. *Reinventing Africa: Museums, Material Culture and Popular Imagination in Late Victorian and Edwardian England*. New Haven: Yale University Press, 1994.

Corbin, Alain. 'Cris et chuchotements' and 'Le secret de l'individu', *Histoire de la vie privée* 4. De la Révolution à la Grande Guerre. Sous la direction de Michelle Perrot. Paris: Seuil, 1987.

Corbin, Alain. *Time, Desire and Horror: Towards a History of the Senses*. Cambridge: Polity, 1995.

Corbin, Alain. *The Life of an Unknown: The Rediscovered World of a Clog Maker in Nineteenth-Century France*. Translated by Arthur Goldhammar. New York: Columbia University Press, 2001.

Curtis Jr., L. Perry. *Jack the Ripper and the London Press*. New Haven: Yale University Press, 2001.

Daniel, Malcolm. '"Divine Perfection": The Daguerreotype in Europe and America'. *The Metropolitan Museum of Art Bulletin*, New Series, 56/4 (spring 1999): 40–6.

Darnton, Robert. 'History of Reading'. In *New Perspectives on Historical Writing*. Edited by Peter Burke. Cambridge: Polity, 1991.

Davis, John A. 'Italy'. *War for the Public Mind: Political Censorship in Nineteenth-Century Europe*. Edited by Robert J. Goldstein, 81–124. Westport, CT: Greenwood Publishing, 2000.

Decker, Hannah S. 'Freud's "Dora" Case: The Crucible of the Psychoanalytic Concept of Transference'. *Freud: Conflict and Culture*. Edited by Michael S. Roth, 105–16. New York: Alfred A. Knopf, 1998.

Delbourg-Delphis, Marylène. *Masculin singulier: Le dandysme et son histoire*. Paris: Hachette, 1985.

Derry, T. K. and Williams, Trevor I. *A Short History of Technology from the Earliest Times to A. D. 1900*. London: Oxford University Press, 1960.

Docker, John. *Postmodernism and Popular Culture: A Cultural History*. Cambridge: Cambridge University Press, 1994.

Eley, Geoff. *Forging Democracy: The History of the Left in Europe, 1850–2000*. Oxford: Oxford University Press, 2002.

Elliot, J. H. *Berlioz*. London: J. M. Dent & Sons, 1946.

Elomaa, Hanna. 'Maalta kaupunkiin'. In *Perhekirja: Eurooppalaisen perheen historia*. Helsinki: Tammi, 1998.

Ferris, David. *Silent Urns: Romanticism, Hellenism, Modernity*. Stanford: Stanford University Press, 2000.

Forsström, Riikka. *Possible Worlds: The Idea of Happiness in the Utopian Vision of Louis-Sébastien Mercier*. Helsinki: Finnish Literature Society, 2002.

Fraser, W. Hamish. *History of British Trade Unionism, 1700–1988*. Basingstoke: Palgrave, 1999.

Frayling, Christopher. 'The House That Jack Built: Some Stereotypes of the Rapist in the History of Popular Culture'. In *Rape: An Historical and Cultural Enquiry*. Edited by Sylvana Tomaselli and Roy Porter, 174–215. Oxford: Blackwell, 1989.

Friedberg, Anne. *Window Shopping: Cinema and the Postmodern*. Los Angeles and Berkeley: University of California Press, 1993.

Frigyesi, Judit. *Béla Bartók and Turn-of-the-Century Budapest*. Berkeley: University of California Press, 1998.

Frisby, David. 'The *Flâneur* in Social Theory'. In *The Flâneur*. Edited by Keith Tester, 81–110. London: Routledge, 1994.

Geertz, Clifford. *The Interpretation of Cultures: Selected Essays*. New York: Basic Books, 1973.

Gerhard, Anselm. *The Urbanization of Opera: Music Theater in Paris in the Nineteenth Century*. Translated by Mary Whittal. Chicago: University of Chicago Press, 2000.

Gianaris, Nicholas V. *Geopolitical and Economic Changes in the Balkan Countries*. Westport, CT: Praeger, 1996.

Grey, Thomas S. 'Wagner's *Die Meistersinger* as National Opera (1868–

1945)'. In *Music and German National Identity*. Edited by Celia Appelgate and Pamela Potter, 78–104. Chicago: University of Chicago Press, 2002.

Gronow, Jukka. *Sociology of Taste*. London: Routledge, 1997.

Gronow, Pekka and Saunio, Ilpo. *An International History of the Record Industry*. Translated from the Finnish by Christopher Moseley. London: Cassell, 1999.

Gunning, Tom. 'An Aesthetic of Astonishment: Early Film and the (In)credulous Spectator'. In *Film Theory: Critical Concepts in Media and Cultural Studies*. Edited by Philip Simpson, Andrew Utterson and K. J. Shepherdson. Vol. 3. London: Routledge, 2004.

Hagen, Rose-Marie and Hagen, Rainer. *Goya: 1746–1828*. Cologne: Taschen, 2003.

Häggman, Kai. *Perheen vuosisata: Perheen ihanne ja sivistyneistön elämäntapa 1800-luvun Suomessa*. Helsinki: Finnish Literature Society, 1994.

Hammond, J. R. '*The Time Machine* as a First Novel: Myth and Allegory in Wells's Romance'. In *H. G. Wells's Perennial Time Machine*. Edited by George Slusser, Patrick Parrinder and Danièle Chatelain, 3–11. Athens: University of Georgia Press, 2001.

Hansen, Miriam. 'Early Silent Cinema: Whose Public Sphere?' *New German Critique* 29, The Origins of Mass Culture: The Case of Imperial Germany (1871–1918); (spring–summer 1983): 147–84.

Hapuli, Ritva. *Nykyajan sininen kukka: Olavi Paavolainen ja nykyaika*. Helsinki: Finnish Literature Society, 1995.

Harrington, Ralph. 'The Railway Accident: Trains, Trauma, and Technological Crises in Nineteenth-Century Britain'. *Traumatic Pasts: Studies in History, Psychiatry, and Trauma in the Modern Age*. Edited by Mark S. Micale and Paul Lerner, 31–56. Cambridge: Cambridge University Press, 2001.

Harsin, Jill. *Barricades: The War of the Streets in Revolutionary Paris, 1830–1848*. New York: Palgrave, 2002.

Held, Jutta. 'Francisco de Goya: Die Gemälde'. *Zeitschrift für Kunstgeschichte* 28/3 (1965): 229–57.

Higonnet, Anne. 'Real Fashion: Clothes Unmake the Working Woman'. In *Spectacles of Realism: Gender, Body, Genre*. Edited by Margaret Cohen and Christopher Prendergast, 137–62. Minneapolis: University of Minnesota Press, 1995.

Hill, C. P. *British Economic and Social History, 1700–1982*. Fifth edition. London: Arnold, 1985.

Hirn, Sven. *Kuvat kulkevat: Kuvallisten esitysten perinne ja elävien kuvien 12 ensimmäistä vuotta Suomessa*. Helsinki: Finnish Film Foundation, 1981.

Histoire de la France littéraire. Vol. 3. Edited by Patrick Berthier and Michel Jarrety. Paris: Presses Universitaires de Paris, 2006.

Hobsbawm, Eric J. 'The Machine Breakers'. *Past & Present* 1 (1952): 57–70.

Hobsbawm, Eric J. *The Age of Revolution 1789–1848*. New York: Mentor, 1962.

Hobsbawm, Eric J. *Industry and Empire: From 1750 to the Present Day*. Harmondsworth: Penguin, 1969.

Hobsbawm, Eric J. *Nations and Nationalism since 1780. Programme, Myth, Reality*. Second edition. Cambridge: Cambridge University Press, 1992.

Howe, Michael J. A. *Genius Explained*. Cambridge: Cambridge University Press, 1999.

Howkins, Alun. 'Agrarian Histories and Agricultural Revolution'. In *Historical Controversies and Historians*. Edited by William Lamont, 81–92. London: UCL Press, 1998.

Huet, Marie-Hélène. 'Chateaubriand and the Politics of (Im)mortality'. *Diacritics* 30/3 (fall 2000): 28–39.

Huhtamo, Erkki. 'Ennen broadcastingia'. *Lähikuva* 1 (1992): 6–17.

Huhtamo, Erkki. 'From Kaleidoscomaniac to Cybernerd: Notes toward an Archaeology of the Media'. *Leonardo* 30/3 (1997): 221–4.

Huhtamo, Erkki. *Fantasmagoria: Elävän kuvan arkeologiaa*. Helsinki: BTJ Kirjastopalvelu, 2000.

Immonen, Kari. 'Uusi kulttuurihistoria'. In *Kulttuurihistoria. Johdatus tutkimukseen*, 20–5. Edited by Kari Immonen and Maarit Leskelä-Kärki. Helsinki: Finnish Literature Society, 2001.

Inglis, Brian. *Poverty and the Industrial Revolution*. London: Panther, 1972.

Inglis, Fred. *Delicious History of the Holiday*. London: Routledge, 2000.

Isaacson, Joel. 'Constable, Duranty, Mallarmé, Impressionism, Plein Air, and Forgetting'. *The Art Bulletin* 76/3 (September 1994): 427–50.

Isham, Howard F. *Image of the Sea: Oceanic Consciousness in the Romantic Century*. New York: Peter Lang, 2004.

Jennings, Jeremy. 'The *Déclaration des droits de l'homme et du citoyen* and Its Critics in France: Reaction and *Idéologie*'. *The Historical Journal* 35/4 (December 1992): 839–59.

Jokisalo, Jouko. 'Ernst Rudorff, esteettinen sivilisaatiokritiikki ja Saksan luonnonsuojeluliikkeen alkukehitys'. In *Luonnonsuojeluajattelusta ympäristökasvatukseen*. Edited by Jouko Jokisalo, Timo Järvikoski and Kari Väyrynen. Oulu: Ecocenter and University of Oulu, 1995.

Kaartinen, Marjo. 'Toinen – vieras. Näkökulmia kolonialistisen toiseuden tutkimukseen'. In *Kulttuurihistoria: Johdatus tutkimukseen*. Edited by Kari Immonen and Maarit Leskelä-Kärki. Helsinki: Finnish Literature Society, 2001.

Kaartinen, Marjo. 'Public and Private: Challenges in the Study of Early Modern Women's Lives'. In *Time Frames. Negotiating Cultural History*. Edited by Anu Korhonen and Kirsi Tuohela. Cultural History – Kulttuurihistoria 1. Turku: Department of Cultural History, 2002.

Kallioniemi, Kari. 'Porvarillisen populaarikulttuurin aikakausi'. In Kari Kallioniemi and Hannu Salmi, *Porvariskodista maailmankylään: Populaarikulttuurin historiaa*. Second edition. Turku: University of Turku, 1995.

Kiberd, Declan: 'Anarchist Attitudes: Oscar Wilde', *The Wilde Years. Oscar Wilde & The Art of His Time*. Edited and with text by Tomoko Sato and Lionel Lambourne. London: Barbican Art Galleries, 2000.

Kirby, Lynne. 'Male Hysteria and Early Cinema'. *Camera Obscura: A Journal of Feminism and Film Theory* 17 (1988): 113–31.

Klinge, Matti. *Idylli ja uhka. Topeliuksen aatteita ja politiikkaa*. Porvoo: WSOY, 1998.

Klinge, Matti. *Kaukana ja kotona*. Translated by Marketta Klinge. Espoo: Schildts, 1997.

Koivunen, Anu. 'Näkyvä nainen ja 'suloinen pyörrytys': Naiset tähtinä ja tähtien kuluttajina 1920-luvun suomalaisessa elokuvajournalismissa'. In *Vampyyrinainen ja Kenkkuinniemen sauna. Suomalainen kaksikymmenluku ja modernin mahdollisuus*. Edited by Tapio Onnela. Helsinki: Finnish Literature Society, 1992.

Koivunen, Leila. *Visualizing Africa in Nineteenth-Century British Travel Accounts*. New York: Routledge, 2008.

Koppen, Erwin. 'Wagnerismus – Begriff und Phänomen'. In *Richard-Wagner-Handbuch*. Edited by Ulrich Müller and Peter Wapnewski. Stuttgart: Kröner, 1986.

Koselleck, Reinhart, et al. 'Volk, Nation, Nationalismus, Masse'. In *Geschichtliche Grundbegriffe: Historisches Lexikon zur politisch-sozialen Sprache in Deutschland*, edited by Otto Brunner, Werner Conze and Reinhart Koselleck, 141–431. Vol. 7. Stuttgart: E. Klett, 1978.

Kostiainen, Auvo. 'Massaturismin historiallinen syntymä'. In *Mikä maa, mikä valuutta: Matkakirja turismin historiaan*. Edited by Auvo Kostiainen and Katariina Korpela. Turku: University of Turku, Department of History, 1995.

Kriegel, Lara. 'Narrating the Subcontinent in 1851: India at the Crystal Palace'. In *The Great Exhibition of 1851: New Interdisciplinary Essays*. Edited by Louise Purbrick, 146–78. Manchester: Manchester University Press, 2001.

Kroen, Sheryl. *Politics and Theater: The Crisis of Legitimacy in Restoration France, 1815–1830*. Los Angeles: University of California Press, 2000.

Krüger, Arnd. 'The Unfinished Symphony: A History of the Olympic Games from Coubertin to Samaranch'. In *International Politics of Sport in the Twentieth Century*. Edited by James Riordan and Arnd Krüger, 3–27. London: Spon Press, 1999.

Kumar, Krishan. *Utopia and Anti-Utopia in Modern Times*. Oxford: Blackwell, 1987.

Larson, Susan and Woods, Eva. 'Visualizing Spanish Modernity: Introduction', 1–23. In *Visualizing Spanish Modernity*. Edited by Susan Larson and Eva Woods. Oxford: Berg Publishers, 2005.

Lawes, Kim. *Paternalism and Politics: The Revival of Paternalism in Early Nineteenth-Century Britain*. Basingstoke: Palgrave, 2000.

Lewis, Brian. *Middlemost and the Milltowns: Bourgeois Culture and Politics in Early Industrial England*. Stanford: Stanford University Press, 2001.

Lilley, Samuel. 'Technological Progress and the Industrial Revolution 1700–1914'. In *The Fontana Economic History of Europe, the Industrial Revolution*. Editor: Carlo M. Cipolla. London: Collins/Fontana Books, 1977.

Litzen, Veikko. 'Kulttuurihistoria on kokonaisvaltaisuutta korostava historia', 7–17. In *Mitä kulttuurihistoria on?* Edited by Kari Immonen. Second edition. Turku: University of Turku, 1981.

Litzmann, Berthold. *Clara Schumann: An Artist's Life*. Vol. 1. Based on Material Found in Diaries and Letters, trans. Grace E. Hadow. London: Macmillan, 1913.

Loeb, Lori Anne. *Consuming Angels: Advertising and Victorian Women*. New York: Oxford University Press, 1994.

Löfgren, Orvar. *On Holiday: A History of Vacationing*. Berkeley: University of California Press, 1999.

McClintock, Anne. *Imperial Leather: Race, Gender and Sexuality in the Colonial Contest*. New York: Routledge, 1995.

McGowan, Christopher. *Rail, Steam, and Speed: The Rocket and the Birth of Steam Locomotion*. New York: Columbia University Press, 2004.

McQuire, Scott. *Visions of Modernity: Representation, Memory, Time and Space in the Age of the Camera*. London: Sage, 1998.

McWilliam, Rohan. *Popular Politics in Nineteenth-Century England*. London: Routledge, 1998.

Magner, Lois N. *A History of the Life Sciences*. Third edition, revised and expanded. London: CRC Press, 2002.

Magherini, Graziella. *La Sindrome di Stendhal*. Florence: Ponte Alle Grazie, 1989.

Malečková, Jitka. 'The Emancipation of Women for the Benefit of the Nation: The Czech Women's Movement'. In *Women's Emancipation Movements in the Nineteenth Century: A European Perspective*. Edited by Sylvia Paletschek and Bianka Petrow-Ennker, 167–88. Stanford: Stanford University Press, 2004.

Marchand, Suzanne. 'Ancients and Moderns in German Museums'. In *Museums and Memory*. Edited by Susan A. Crane. Stanford, CA: Stanford University Press, 2000.

Marinetti, Amelita. 'Death, Resurrection, and Fall in Dumas' Comte de Monte-Cristo'. *The French Review* 50/2 (December 1976): 260–9.

Markkola, Pirjo. *Työläiskodin synty: Tamperelaiset työläisperheet ja yhteiskunnallinen kysymys 1870-luvulta 1910-luvulle*. Helsinki: Finnish Literature Society, 1994.

Marsh, Josh. 'Spectacle'. *A Companion to Victorian Literature and Culture*. Edited by Herbert F. Tucker, 276–88. Oxford: Blackwell, 1999.

Martin-Fugier, Anne. 'Les rites de la vie privée bourgeoise'. In *Histoire de la vie privée*. Vol. 4. De la Révolution à la Grande Guerre. Sous la direction de Michelle Perrot. Paris: Seuil, 1987.

Marx, Leo. *The Machine in the Garden: Technology and the Pastoral Ideal in America*. New York: Oxford University Press, 1964.

Mayer, David. 'Introduction'. In *Playing Out the Empire: Ben-Hur and Other Toga Plays and Films, 1883–1908. A Critical Anthology*. Edited with Introductions and Notes by David Mayer and an essay on the incidental music for toga dramas by Katherine Preston, 1–22. Oxford: Clarendon Press, 1994.

Melton, James Van Horn. *Rise of the Public in Enlightenment Europe*. Cambridge: Cambridge University Press, 2001.

Metzner, Paul. *Crescendo of the Virtuoso: Spectacle, Skill, and Self-Promotion in Paris during the Age of Romanticism*. Berkeley: University of California Press, 1998.

Millington, Barry. *Wagner*. Second printing, with corrections. Princeton, NJ: Princeton University Press, 1998.

Moore, Dafydd R. 'The Critical Response to Ossian's Romantic Bequest'. *English Romanticism and the Celtic World*. Edited by Gerard Carruthers, 38–53. Cambridge: Cambridge University Press, 2003.

Morse, Marcia. 'Feminist Aesthetics and the Spectrum of Gender'. *Philosophy East and West* 42/2 (April 1992): 287–95.

Mumford, Lewis. *The Culture of Cities*. New York: Harcourt Brace & Company, 1938.

Mumford, Lewis. *Technics and Civilization*. New York: Harcourt Brace Jovanivich, 1963.

Mustakallio, Marja. *'Teen nyt paljon musiikkia': Fanny Henselin (1805–1847) toiminta modernisoituvassa musiikkikulttuurissa*. Turku: Åbo Akademi University Press, 2003.

Nash, Mary. 'The Rise of the Women's Movement in Nineteenth-Century Spain'. In *Women's Emancipation Movements in the Nineteenth Century: A European Perspective*. Edited by Sylvia Paletschek and Bianka Petrow-Ennker, 243–62. Stanford: Stanford University Press, 2004.

O'Halloran, Clare. 'Irish Re-Creations of the Gaelic Past: The Challenge of Macpherson's Ossian'. *Past and Present* 124 (August 1989): 69–95.

Ollila, Anne. *Jalo velvollisuus: Virkanaisena 1800-luvun lopun Suomessa*. Helsinki: Finnish Literature Society, 1998.

Ollila, Anne. *Aika ja elämä: Aikakäsitys 1800-luvun lopussa*. Helsinki: Finnish Literature Society, 2000.

Ollila, Anne. 'Questioning the Categories of Private and Public: Salons in the Nordic Countries in the Nineteenth Century'. In *Time Frames. Negotiating Cultural History*. Edited by Anu Korhonen and Kirsi Tuohela. Cultural History – Kulttuurihistoria 1. Turku: Department of Cultural History, 2002.

Onnela, Tapio. 'Kuvaan kiinnittyvä valta: Valokuvaus tiedon ja kontrollin kentässä'. *Lähikuva* 1 (1993): 19–28.

Paalumäki, Heli. '"Imagine a Good Day" – Bertrand de Jouvenel's Idea of Possible Futures in the Context of Fictitious and Historical Narratives'.

Ennen & nyt, Vol. 1: The Papers of the Nordic Conference on the History of Ideas. Helsinki, 2001.

Palmgren, Raoul. *Kaupunki ja tekniikka Suomen kirjallisuudessa: Kuvauslinjoja ennen ja jälkeen tulenkantajien*. Helsinki: Finnish Literature Society, 1989.

Palti, Elías José. 'The Nation as a Problem: Historians and the "National Question"'. *History and Theory* 40/3 (October 2001): 324–46.

Pattison, George. *Kierkegaard, Religion, and the Nineteenth-Century Crisis of Culture*. Cambridge: Cambridge University Press, 2002.

Perrot, Michelle. 'La vie de famille'. In *Histoire de la vie privée*. Vol 4. De la Révolution à la Grande Guerre. Sous la direction de Michelle Perrot. Paris: Seuil, 1987.

Pomeranz, Kenneth. *Great Divergence: China, Europe and the Making of the Modern World Economy*. Princeton, NJ: Princeton University Press, 2000.

Poster, Mark. 'The Question of Agency: Michel de Certeau and the History of Consumerism'. *Diacritics* 22/2 (summer 1992): 94–107.

Pulla, Armas J. *Tammikuun ensimmäinen 1900*. Helsinki: Otava, 1981.

Quine, Maria Sophia. *Italy's Social Revolution: Charity and Welfare from Liberalism to Fascism*. Basingstoke: Palgrave, 2002.

Reich, Nancy B. *Clara Schumann: The Artist and the Woman*. Revised edition. Ithaca, NY: Cornell University Press, 2001.

Reid, Donald Malcolm. *Whose Pharaohs?: Archaeology, Museums and Egyptian Identity from Napolean to World War I* . Berkeley: University of California Press, 2002.

Ringbom, Sixten: 'Guérin, Delacroix and "The Liberty"'. *The Burlington Magazine* 110/782 (May 1968): 270, 273–5.

Rose, Bob. 'Projection'. In *The Focal Encyclopedia of Photography: Digital Imaging, Theory and Applications, History, and Science*. Fourth edition. Edited by Michael R. Peres, 803–6. Burlington, MA: Focal Press, 2007.

Rosengren, Carola. *Unelma kesästä: Huvilakulttuuria 1910-luvun Ruissalossa*. Turku: k&h, 2003.

Sadoul, Georges. *Georges Méliès*. Translated into Finnish by Satu Laaksonen. Helsinki: Finnish Film Achive, 1985.

Said, Edward W. *Orientalism*. Routledge & Kegan Paul, London 1978.

Salmi, Hannu. *'Atoomipommilla kuuhun!' Tekniikan mentaalihistoriaa*. Helsinki: Edita, 1996.

Salmi, Hannu. *Imagined Germany. Richard Wagner's National Utopia.* German Life and Civilization. General editor: Jost Hermand. New York: Peter Lang, 1999.

Salmi, Hannu. *Wagner and Wagnerism in Nineteenth-Century Sweden, Finland, and the Baltic Provinces: Reception, Enthusiasm, Cult.* Eastman Studies in Music. Rochester, NY: University of Rochester Press, 2005.

Savolainen, Irma. *Taiteilijoita, käsityöläisiä ja taivaanrannanmaalareita: Turkulaiset valokuvaajat vuoteen 1918.* Turku: Turku Provincal Museum, 1992.

Scambler, Graham. *Sport and Society: History, Power and Culture.* Maidenhead, Berkshire: Open University Press, 2005.

Schivelbusch, Wolfgang. *The Railway Journey: Trains and Travel in the nineteenth Century.* Translated from the German by Anselm Hollo. Oxford: Blackwell, 1980.

Schivelbusch, Wolfgang. *The Railway Journey: The Industrialization and Perception of Time and Space.* Berkeley: University of California Press, 1987.

Schivelbusch, Wolfgang. *Disenchanted Night: The Industrialization of Light in the Nineteenth Century.* Translated from the German by Angela Davies. Berkeley: University of California Press, 1988.

Schlüppmann, Heide. 'Kinosucht'. *Frauen und Film* 30 (October 1982): 45–52.

Schulz, David. 'Redressing Oscar: Performance and the Trials of Oscar Wilde'. *The Drama Review* 40/2 (summer 1996): 37–59.

Schwartz, Vanessa R. *Spectacular Realities: Early Mass Culture in Fin-de-Siècle Paris.* Berkeley: University of California Press, 1998.

Shubert, Adrian. *Social History of Modern Spain.* London: Routledge, 1990.

Sjögren, Lars. *Sigmund Freud: Elämä ja teokset.* Translated by Leena Nivala. Porvoo: WSOY, 1991.

Smith, Anthony D. *Nationalism and Modernism: A Critical Survey of Recent Theories of Nations and Nationalism.* London: Routledge, 1998.

Smith, Anthony D. *Nationalism: Theory, Ideology, History.* Key Concepts. Cambridge: Polity, 2001.

Starr Guilloton, Doris. 'Toward a New Freedom: Rahel Varnhagen and the German Women Writers before 1848'. In *Woman as Mediatrix: Essays on Nineteenth-Century European Women Writers.* Vol. 10. Edited by Avriel H. Goldberger. New York: Greenwood Press, 1987.

Sulkunen, Irma. 'Naisten järjestäytyminen ja kaksijakoinen kansalaisuus'.

In *Kansa liikkeessä*. Edited by Risto Alapuro, Ilkka Liikanen, Kerstin Smeds, Henrik Stenius. Helsinki: Kirjayhtymä, 1987.

Summerfield, Penny. 'Patriotism and Empire: Music-Hall Entertainment 1870–1914', In *Imperialism and Popular Culture*. Edited by John M. MacKenzie, 17–48. Manchester: Manchester University Press, 1986.

Sussman, Herbert L. *Victorians and the Machine: The Literary Response to Technology*. Cambridge, Mass.: Harvard University Press, 1968.

Syrjämaa, Taina. *Constructing Unity, Living in Diversity: A Roman Decade*. Annales Academiae Scientiarum Fennicae 344. Helsinki: Academia Scientiarum Fennica, 2006.

Talonen, Jyrki. 'Poisjääntejä ja boikotteja olympialiikkeessä 1896–1984'. In *Urheilu ja historia. Kansakunnan identiteetiksi, yhteiskunnan vaikuttajaksi, joukkojen harrastukseksi*. Edited by Vesa Vares, 123–46. Turku: Turku Historical Society, 1997.

Teich, Mikuláš and Porter, Roy: 'Introduction'. In *Fin de siècle and its Legacy*. Edited by Mikuláš Teich and Roy Porter, 1–9. Cambridge: Cambridge University Press, 1990.

Thomis, Malcolm I. *The Luddites. Machine-Breaking in Regency England*. Newton Abbot Hamden, CT: Archon Books, 1970.

Todd, R. Larry. *Mendelssohn: A Life in Music*. Oxford: Oxford University Press, 2003.

Tuohela, Kirsi. 'Being ill in the Past: Historicizing Women's Experience of Body and Illness'. In *Time Frames. Negotiating Cultural History*. Edited by Anu Korhonen and Kirsi Tuohela. Cultural History – Kulttuurihistoria 1. Turku: Department of Cultural History, 2002.

Tuohela, Kirsi and Korhonen, Anu. 'Final Comments: Recoding Culture'. In *Time Frames. Negotiating Cultural History*. Edited by Anu Korhonen and Kirsi Tuohela. Cultural History – Kulttuurihistoria 1. Turku: Department of Cultural History, 2002.

Uimonen, Minna. *Hermostumisen aikakausi: Neuroosit 1800- ja 1900-lukujen vaihteen suomalaisessa lääketieteessä*. Helsinki: Finnish Literature Society, 1999.

Varikas, Eleni. 'National and Gender Identity in Turn-of-the-Century Greece'. In *Women's Emancipation Movements in the Nineteenth Century: A European Perspective*. Edited by Sylvia Paletschek and Bianka Petrow-Ennker, 263–79. Stanford: Stanford University Press, 2004.

Väyrynen, Kari. 'Omistusoikeus ja luonto: klassisen teorian ongelmia'. In

Luonnonsuojeluajattelusta ympäristökasvatukseen. Edited by Jouko Jokisalo, Timo Järvikoski and Kari Väyrynen. Oulu: Ecocenter and University of Oulu, 1995.

Virtanen, Keijo. *Kulttuurihistoria – tie kokonaisvaltaiseen historiaan.* Turku: University of Turku, 1987.

Vrettos, Athena. *Somatic Fictions: Imagining Illness in Victorian Culture.* Stanford: Stanford University Press, 1995.

Wakefield, David. 'Chateaubriand's "Atala" as a Source of Inspiration in Nineteenth-Century Art'. *The Burlington Magazine* 120/898 (January 1978): 13–24.

Waller, John. *Real Oliver Twist.* Cambridge: Icon Books, 2007.

Ward, Peter. *Kitsch in Sync: A Consumer's Guide to Bad Taste.* London: Plexus, 1991.

Wiener, Martin J. *Men of Blood: Violence, Manliness, and Criminal Justice in Victorian England.* Cambridge: Cambridge University Press, 2004.

Wilson Kimber, Marian. 'The "Suppression" of Fanny Mendelssohn: Rethinking Feminist Biography'. *nineteenth-Century Music* 26/2 (autumn 2002): 113–29.

Young, Allan. *Harmony of Illusions: Inventing Post-Traumatic Stress Disorder.* Princeton, NJ: Princeton University Press, 1997.

Index

CPSIA information can be obtained
at www.ICGtesting.com
Printed in the USA
BVOW10s2111140817
492053BV00010B/76/P